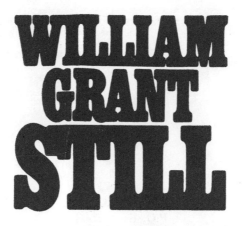

WILLIAM GRANT STILL

AND THE FUSION OF CULTURES IN AMERICAN MUSIC

ROBERT BARTLETT HAAS (EDITOR) AND
PAUL HAROLD SLATTERY, VERNA ARVEY,
WILLIAM GRANT STILL, LOUIS AND
ANNETTE KAUFMAN, WITH INTRODUCTIONS
BY HOWARD HANSON AND FREDERICK HALL.

BLACK SPARROW PRESS - LOS ANGELES - 1972

Black Sparrow Press
P.O. Box 25603
Los Angeles, California
90025

GL

LIBRARY OF CONGRESS CATALOGING IN PUBLICATION DATA

Haas, Robert Bartlett, comp.
    William Grant Still and the fusion of cultures in American music.

    Bibliography: p.
        1. Still, William Grant, 1895-   Works.
I. Title.
ML410.S855H2   780'.92'4   72.5955
 ISBN 0-87685-149-9
 ISBN 0-87685-150-2 (autographed ed.)

DEDICATION

For my father and mother:

WILLIAM GRANT STILL SR.
1871 - 1895

CARRIE LENA FAMBRO STILL SHEPPERSON
1871 - 1927

CONTENTS

encyclopedia

William Grant Still's place in music history as the dean of America's Negro composers is assured. It is a proud distinction, but it is not enough. For Still is, above all, an American composer, interpreting the spiritual values of his own land through his own brand of personal genius.

He has been able to do this because he is not only a creator but a warm, human being with a deep affection and compassion for people. It is natural that his music should be forthright, direct, and without artifice. Whether in the poignant, emotion-filled slow movement of the *Afro-American Symphony* or the hard-driving chants and dances from his great ballet, *Sahdji*, it is always people-music. His music does what, I believe, most of us feel music should do, it communicates.

I have known William Grant Still as a close friend and have admired him as a colleague for almost a half-century. I have had the privilege of conducting most of his major works, many of them for the first time. I recall the excitement of conducting the Scherzo from his *Afro-American Symphony* in Berlin with the Berlin Philharmonic Orchestra in the early thirties and the vociferous demand of that conservative audience that we repeat it—which we did! All of which tends to prove that music which has its roots deep in the human heart is the most personal, the most national, and also, the most universal.

HOWARD HANSON

One writer has said that music is one of God's choicest gifts to mankind, and that American Negro Music is one of the nation's richest gifts to the civilization of our time. For many decades the only voice that the American Negro had was his music. William Grant Still, Dean of American Composers, has made this voice to be heard and respected throughout the world. His genius is one of a rare and peculiar kind. Everything that he touches he adorns, whether his is a simple melodic line, or a massive structure of operatic or symphonic architecture.

Still writes in every medium of musical expression with a power that is undergirded by a spirit of great humility and honest dedication. It is such a spirit that causes him to rise above the technical and creative skills of musical composition, over which he has complete mastery, and give forth utterances that "lift a race from wood and stone to Christ." What he has done and is doing for American Negro Music is inestimable.

In writing for entertainment, he displays a dignity so necessary to the honest evaluation of music in this category; in religious writing he shows a depth of consecration; in larger forms, instrumental and vocal, he creates a new freshness without destroying the strength and beauty of the old.

American Negro Music owes Still an eternal debt of gratitude; the voice of the world is ready to exclaim, in clarion effulgence, "Hats off, gentlemen, a genius."

FREDERICK HALL

AN APPRECIATION FOR NOW

When Miss Mary D. Hudgins, writing in the *Arkansas Gazette*, called William Grant Still "the Dean of American Negro Composers," she thought this might be overly dramatic. Now we know her characterization was quite right.

No other Negro composer (in fact few other composers after the Romantic era) has set such a consistent musical path for himself and followed it. Those who preceded him had their work to do but did not achieve his breadth: Burleigh's accompaniments for Spirituals made them more effective; Dett wrote some choral works in larger scale utilizing folk sources; Clarence White dealt with folk materials, too, but not always—and when he moved away from them, he managed to produce only pleasant salon-pieces.

Therefore, William Grant Still knew he too had work to do. His first course was to take up the Negroid idiom and elevate it to symphonic form—not the folk themes but the idiom. Then he branched out to use in his music all the ethnic strains which combine in his own background. Thus he reached a distinctive personal idiom which has traced out the fusion of musical cultures in America.

In the earlier part of his life Still was not acquainted with the Negro idiom at all. He had to learn it as he learned other things. Someone is always trying to find out what Spirituals he used in the *Afro-American Symphony*. None. Only themes he has created himself. And, although at one time he did something with this Negro idiom, he used it as he used everything else, then left it behind, shutting out nothing new. Still went into popular music to learn what he could, but he never let it control him. The European and American *avant-gardists* tried to claim him, but he is an independent thinker, not a musical faddist. He has always spoken for himself. He doesn't disclaim the right of others to do what they want, but for him the consistent path was devoted craftsmanship, form, melody, beautiful sounds—and the exploration of the racial strains which fuse in his own background. Father: Scotch, Negro and Choctaw Indian. Mother: Negro, Indian, Spanish and Irish. On his own (on occasion) he has added the Creole idiom of French Louisiana and the Hebraic as he learned it through his commission undertaken for the Park Avenue Synagogue.

1

Then, of course, there is the part of Still that combines all of this—the "American" Still. And the part which floats above to touch only on universals, where the idiom is William Grant Still alone with his God and on his very personal inward adventure with music.

Because of Still's encompassing perspective and personal security, the "Black" music movement, the "soul music" tradition, hasn't diverted him. He sees it as limiting and essentially racist. The militants claim he is writing "Eur-American", not "Afro-America" music, but this is not an historically accurate statement. Hale Smith, Ulysses Kay, Arthur Cunningham, Olly Wilson, and others, Black composers, *avant-garde* to a greater or lesser degree, all recognize Still as a pioneer who has increased the stature of Negro music. And some, like Smith and Kay, have not hesitated to say openly that their way was made easier because of William Grant Still.

Although the music of William Grant Still is steadily played in this country, there is an enormous body of his work which hasn't yet been heard and which awaits a conductor who does for Still what Sir Thomas Beecham did for Delius. Other conductors may someday discover their reputations rest on what they didn't play rather than on what they played.

Meanwhile, this book is an invitation to all men of good will everywhere, to understand and appreciate the musical legacy of William Grant Still, "Dean of American Negro Composers" and citizen of the universe.

R. B. H.

2

THE STORY OF WILLIAM GRANT STILL

William Grant Still was born in Woodville, Mississippi, May 11, 1895, the son of William Grant and Carrie Lena (Fambro) Still. Both parents were teachers with a college education. "His father taught music at the Agricultural and Mechanical college of Alabama and died when his son, William, was but three months old."[1] Having relatives in Arkansas, the young widow Still brought her tiny son to Little Rock and accepted a teaching job in that community, a position she was to hold until her death in 1927. During the next few years, the musical background of young William was to be enriched through the influence of his maternal grandmother. Verna Arvey comments on this exposure to the music of Still's people:

> While his grandmother worked about their house, she sang hymns and spirituals. "Little David, Play on Yo' Harp" was one of her favorites. Thus he grew up with the songs of his people, and grew to love the old hymns, which he plays today with the addition of such exquisite harmonies that they assume unsuspected beauty. A communal habit of the childhood days was that of serenading. It was pleasant to be awakened from slumber by such sweet sounds. He has always deplored the passing of that custom.[2]

The next enriching factor to enter the life of young William Still was his stepfather, Charles B. Shepperson. Hudgins describes this second marriage of Mrs. Still.

> When her son was yet a small boy she married Charles B. Shepperson, a railway postal clerk, possessed by a deep love of music, particularly opera. Fortunately his salary permitted him to buy a phonograph; and thus enrich the lives of members of his family with a constant stream of the best Red Seal records.[3]

The relationship between William and his stepfather was a positive and rewarding experience. Mr. Shepperson enhanced the boy's musical background by taking the family to the best musi-

---

[1] Mary D. Hudgins, "An Outstanding Arkansas Composer, William Grant Still", *Arkansas Historical Quarterly*, Winter, 1965, p. 309. In actual fact, Still was six months old.

[2] Verna Arvey, *Studies of Contemporary American Composers: William Grant Still* (New York: J. Fischer and Brother, 1939), p. 9.

[3] Hudgins, *loc. cit.*

cal shows, by singing duets at home, and by discussing with his son the plays and concerts they had attended. The activities mentioned made a significant and highly beneficial contribution to the early life of the composer.

Verna Arvey describes the influence of the composer's mother:

> His mother's determination, good sense, talent and high moral character influenced his life strongly. She was the sort of vital personality who could command attention merely by entering a room. Her students adored her, and learned more from her than from anyone else; so did her young son, for he too was in her classes at school. Here she was stricter with him than anyone else, for she did not want to be accused of favoritism.[4]

At the age of sixteen, William Grant Still was graduated from high school; he was the valedictorian and first honor bearer of his class.[5]

Experiences at Wilberforce University. By the age of sixteen William Still's primary interest was music; he aspired to be a musician and a serious composer. His mother, althought she understood his yearnings, felt that there was no future for a musician, especially a Negro musician; she openly opposed a career in music. Accordingly, the young man was enrolled at Wilberforce University to work toward a Bachelor of Science degree and a career in medicine. Though his heart was not in accord, William respected his mother's wishes; he maintained a slightly above average scholastic record.[6] While at Wilberforce, the aspiring young musician was able to continue his musical pursuits. His first step was to organize a string quartet in which he played the violin; this led to his first experiments with writing arrangements. He learned to play the oboe and the clarinet and became a member of the college band which led to further experiments in the field of orchestration. This important experience is described by Verna Arvey:

> In his capacity as bandleader, he had to learn to play different instruments such as the piccolo and saxophone so that he could teach them to other players. The intimate knowledge of all instruments gained in this fashion has meant much to him in later years, and to his career as an orchestrator.[7]

---

[4] Arvey, *op. cit.*, p. 10.

[5] For detailed coverage of Mr. Still's early life consult "My Arkansas Boyhood" by William Grant Still (see Bibliography) and Verna Arvey's booklet, *op. cit.*

[6] Arvey, *loc. cit.*

[7] *Ibid.*, p. 11.

Some of the teachers at Wilberforce encouraged his musical efforts and it was here that the first recital of Still's compositions was given. This recital included songs and a few band numbers. The recognition accorded him as a result of this successful concert reinforced the young man's desire to devote his life to music. Hudgins comments on this concert and subsequent happenings:

> On one occasion the band offered an entire program of his compositions. But this wasn't enough to satisfy young Still. He quit college and went to work as a professional musician. After several years with commercial units, including that of W. C. Handy, he felt sufficiently financially secure to go back to the classroom.[8]

The unsettled years. Following the years at Wilberforce there came lean, unsettled years; these were years filled with an assortment of experiences that included an unsatisfactory marriage, playing the oboe and 'cello with various orchestras, starving, freezing, working at odd jobs for little money, and a hitch in the U.S. Navy in 1918. Returning home from the Navy, Mr. Still renewed his association with W. C. Handy who had by this time moved his firm to New York City. Verna Arvey comments on this:

> W. C. Handy, father of the Blues, offered him his first job in New York City as an arranger, and as a musician on the road, traveling through large and small Southern towns with Handy's Band.[9]

The field of popular music satisfied him for awhile, but Still's desire to write meaningful, serious music remained with him.

Extended formal training. During the lean years Mr. Still had received a legacy from his father. This legacy was used for further formal training at Oberlin College in Ohio. William first studied theory and the violin. His teachers at Oberlin were so impressed by his talent and his sincerity that a special scholarship was established which would enable him to study composition with Dr. George W. Andrews.[10]

A few years later Still was playing with Eubie Blake's orchestra for the very popular show *Shuffle Along* which was on an extended road trip. Verna Arvey reports on the happenings in Boston:

---

8 Hudgins, *op. cit.*, pp. 310-311..
9 Arvey, *op. cit.*, p. 12.
10 *Ibid.*

5

While *Shuffle Along* was playing in Boston, Still became aware that he could now afford to pay for musical instructions, and filed his application at the New England Conservatory of Music. When he returned for his answer, he was told that George W. Chadwick would teach him free of charge. He protested that he could afford to pay, but generous Chadwick refused to take his money.[11]

After four months of training with Mr. Chadwick, Still returned to New York to accept the position of recording director of the Black Swan Phonograph Company. Through a stroke of good fortune, he learned that Edgar Varese was offering a scholarship in composition to a talented young Negro composer. Still applied for the scholarship, was accepted, and spent the next two years (1923-1925) in the study of composition with the French ultra modernist.[12] Thus came about Still's introduction to Edgar Varese and the Modern idiom. Still's attitude toward his instructors is reported by Verna Arvey:

> When I was groping blindly in my efforts to compose, it was Varese who pointed out to me the way to individual expression and who gave me the opportunity to hear my music played. I shall never forget his kindness, nor that of George W. Chadwick and the instructors at Oberlin.[13]

Hudgins reports on the influence of Varese: "At first Varese made a deep impression on Still, and so inspired, he produced deliberate dissonances. But he soon returned to the more melodic forms of composition." [14]

A career as an arranger. Mr. Still was much in demand as an orchestrator and arranger. Had he chosen to do so, he could have adopted this as his life's work. At various times he worked for Earl Carroll, Artie Shaw, Sophie Tucker, Don Vorhees, and Paul Whiteman.[15] One of the best selling records of all time, Artie Shaw's *Frenesi*, was arranged by Still. As an arranger and conductor he worked for both CBS and Mutual networks. He was given credit by many for the popularity of the "Deep River Hour" which featured Willard Robison on the NBC network. In later

---

[11] *Ibid.*, pp. 12-13.
[12] Madeleine Goss, *'Modern' Music Makers: Contemporary American Composers* (New York: E. P. Dutton and Co., 1952), p. 210.
[13] Arvey, *op. cit.*, p. 13.
[14] Hudgins, *op. cit.*, p. 311.
[15] *Ibid.*, p. 309.

years, on the west coast, he sometimes worked as an arranger for
moving pictures.

Famous "firsts" for William Grant Still. Hudgins submits the
following impressive list:

> Dr. Still's "firsts" are legion. In 1931 his *Afro-American Symphony*
> was heralded as the first major piece of music written by a Negro to
> be played before an American audience. Five years later he was the
> first Negro to conduct an important orchestra, when he picked up the
> baton to direct the Los Angeles Philharmonic in the Hollywood Bowl
> in an evening of his own compositions. In 1955, through conducting
> the New Orleans Philharmonic at Southern University, he became the
> first Negro to conduct a major all white orchestra in the deep south.[16]

Special awards. In 1928 William Grant Still was the recipient
of the second Harmon Award. This award is granted annually by
the Harmon Foundation for the most significant contribution during the year to Negro culture in the United States.[17] Mr. Still was
also the recipient of a 1934 Guggenheim Fellowship which was
twice renewed for periods of six months each.[18] He was commissioned to prepare specific compositions for the League of Composers, Cleveland Orchestra, American Accordionists Association,
New York World's Fair (the theme music for the fair of 1939-
40), and the United States Military Academy band at West-
Point.[19]

Honorary degrees. Five institutions of higher learning have
awarded honorary degrees to Mr. Still as listed:

Wilberforce University	....	Master of Music—1936
Howard University	....	Doctor of Music—1941
Oberlin College	....	Doctor of Music—1947
Bates College	....	Doctor of Letters—1954[20]
University of Arkansas	....	Doctor of Law—1971

The citation which accompanied the Bates College honorary
Doctor of Letters degree read:

---

16 *Ibid.*, p. 312. Correction: Still conducted two of his own pieces at the Hollywood Bowl in 1936. Also, the Los Angeles Philharmonic was already a "major"
orchestra.

17 Arvey, *op. cit.*, p. 17.

18 *Ibid.*, p. 47.

19 Hudgins, *loc. cit.*

20 John Tasker Howard, *Our American Music* (3rd ed.; New York: Thomas Y.
Crowell Co., 1947), p. 466.

Some men have improved race relations through court instruments; others have written flaming books, or moving plays. William Grant Still's contribution has been as a dedicated man who strongly believes that if a Negro's creativeness is of first quality, he will be ranked among the leaders in inter-racial influence. In this endeavor he used the method he knew best—music.[21]

The latter years of Mr. Still. The composer moved to the west coast in 1934 and married Verna Arvey in 1939. This marriage produced two children, Duncan and Judith. Both of the children are college graduates, are married and are launching successful careers of their own. For a period of fourteen years (1939 to 1953) William Grant Still continued to work at a man killing pace. He would put in a work day of from twelve to sixteen hours. Although his commercial work would have been considered more than a full-time occupation, he refused to set aside his most important work, his composition. Eventually. the long hours took their toll and his eyes started to show the strain. In recent years, Mr. Still has accepted a less demanding schedule. However, he still finds time for new compositions plus the continued process of revising and editing older works.

P. H. S.

---

[21] Hudgins, *op. cit.*, p. 312.

THE SYMPHONIC WORKS

INTRODUCTORY NOTE

The purpose of this section is to present a comprehensive portrayal of William Grant Still, the man, his style of musical composition, his compositional philosophy, and his place in the historical style continuum of American music. The *First Symphony* (*The Afro-American*) and the *Fourth Symphony* (*Autochthonous*) have been chosen for study because they represent examples of Mr. Still's highest level of achievement in the field of musical composition. The *Afro-American Symphony* (1930) and *Autochthonous* (1947) will be submitted to analysis and comparison; comparisons will be made in the following areas:

1. Formal structure
2. Harmonic structure and vocabulary
3. Origin of themes and thematic development
4. Factors that unify the symphonies
5. Methods used to obtain variety of expression
6. Orchestration technique
7. Rhythmic devices employed
8. Accomplishment of the tension-release cycle
9. The basic compositional style of the symphonies

William Grant Still is recognized as one of the first Negro composers to attain national and international recognition. His *Afro-American Symphony* has received world-wide acclaim and is considered one of his finest compositions; it is a favorite of the composer. The symphony subtitled *Autochthonous*, written some seventeen years after the *Afro-American*, is also highly regarded. A partial goal of this study is to examine these two symphonies and to point out how they are similar and how they differ.

The gathering and enumeration of a composer's ideas, attitudes, feelings, and compositional philosophy while he is still living can have special value to musicologists of the future, as well as to the interested student of music and music history.

P.H.S.

A COMPREHENSIVE STUDY OF THE
AFRO-AMERICAN SYMPHONY

William Grant Still has informed the writer that a comprehensive study of the *Afro-American Symphony*, which includes a detailed harmonic analysis, has not, to the best of his knowledge, been made. The aim of this chapter is to examine this symphony and to present a clear, concise, and complete picture of the musical devices involved in its composition.

I. GENERAL CONSIDERATIONS

The Creation of The Afro-American Symphony

The composer's intention. "I knew I wanted to write a symphony; I knew that it had to be an *American* work; and I wanted to demonstrate how the *Blues*, so often considered a lowly expression, could be elevated to the highest musical level." The above statement by William Grant Still was submitted to Karl Krueger to be included in the jacket notes for the Society for the Preservation of the American Musical Heritage's recording of *Afro-American Symphony*.[1]

In the text of a speech given to a Composer's Workshop in 1967, Mr. Still gives us further clues concerning his precompositional thought:

> Long before writing this symphony I had recognized the musical value of the *Blues* and had decided to use a theme in the *Blues* idiom as the basis for a major symphonic composition. When I was ready to launch this project I did not want to use a theme some folk singer had already created, but decided to create my own theme in the *Blues* idiom.[2]

The collection of themes. The actual creation of material for the *Afro-American* was taking place for several years prior to 1930. The composer penciled themes in a sketch book over a period of years. These themes were listed in categories such as passion-

---

[1] See p. 168.
[2] Speech to Composer's Workshop, annual convention of National Association of Negro Musicians, Los Angeles, Calif., August 17, 1967.

ate, happy, dramatic, plaintive, and barbaric.

The compositional process. The themes had been collected and the inspiration and motivation for composing were vividly present in the mind and in the heart of the composer; the remaining necessary ingredients were the time and the place to begin the creative activity.

Mr. Still describes this creation:

> It was not until the depression struck that I went jobless long enough to let the Symphony take shape. In 1930, I rented a room in a quiet building not far from my home in New York, and began to work. I devised my own Blues theme (which appears in varied guises throughout the Symphony, as a unifying thread), planned the form, then wrote the entire melody. After that I worked out the harmonies, the various treatments of the theme, and the orchestration.[3]

The addition of program notes and poem fragments. At the time the *Symphony* was written, the composer states that no thought was given to program notes; these were added after the completion of the work, as were the verses from poems by Paul Laurence Dunbar. In 1939, Mr. Still made the following comments concerning these additions:

> I have regretted this step because in this particular instance a program is decidedly inadequate. The program devised at the time, stated that the music portrayed the "sons of the soil," that is, that it offered a composite musical portrait of those Afro-Americans who have not responded completely to the cultural influences of today. It is true that an interpretation of that sort may be read into the music. Nevertheless, one who hears it is quite sure to discover other meanings which are probably broader in their scope.[4]

Excerpts from the poems of Paul Laurence Dunbar precede each movement of the symphony. Each movement is designed to portray a specific emotion and the poetic excerpts serve as an extra-musical means of reinforcing this emotion. To this limited extent, the *Afro-American Symphony* may be described as being "programmatic" in nature.

---

[3] From jacket notes (Krueger), *op. cit.*
[4] Verna Arvey, *William Grant Still: Studies of Contemporary American Composers* (New York: J. Fischer and Brother, 1939), pp. 23-24.

Significant Data

Brief descriptive statement. The *Afro-American Symphony* is a tonal composition in four movements with emphasis placed on the free flow of the melodic line. The use of the *Blues* scale (a nine-tone mode which includes the flatted third and seventh degrees of the regular diatonic scale) permitted extensive usage of melodic nuance. The harmonies are basically simple, but differ from traditional European harmony in that they include an extensive use of added-tone chords. These added-tone chords include the root, third, and fifth along with the sixth, seventh, or ninth. The most used device, however, was the triad (major or minor) with the added minor seventh interval. The "blue" notes in the melodic line and the embellished, piquant harmonies are the major devices that accomplished uniqueness for this composition in 1930.

> . . . *the Afro-American Symphony*, was composed in 1930, dedicated to Irving Schwerke and performed by the Rochester Philharmonic Orchestra in Rochester in 1931 and 1932 and in part under the direction of Dr. Howard Hanson (who introduced it) in Berlin, Stuttgart and Leipzig in 1933. These dates show conclusively that Still's work preceded that of another Negro composer who in 1934 was heralded as having written the *first* Negro symphony.[5]

It is important to note here that this is *probably* the first use of the banjo in a major symphonic work. None of the sources comment on this fact, but both Verna Arvey and William Grant Still are of the opinion that this is the first serious usage of this instrument. In the personal interview of February 12, 1969, both Mr. and Mrs. Still stated that they knew of no attempt to use the banjo in a major composition prior to 1930.[6]

Time breakdown. The following time breakdown is taken from page four of the score of the *Afro-American Symphony*, Fischer Edition No. 0318, with revisions by William Grant Still. (Revision dates impossible to establish.) It is of interest to note that the divisions of this symphony are referred to as Part I, Part II, Part III, and Part IV instead of being referred to as *movements;* also, Mr. Still does not use the terms exposition, development, and recapitulation, but rather the terms Division I, II, and III. This, in a

---

[5] Arvey, *op. cit.,* pp.23-23.
[6] Personal interview: Paul H. Slattery with Verna Arvey and William Grant Still.

13

sense helps to demonstrate his desire to break away from a strict adherence to traditional practices. The time breakdown is as follows:

Part I	7¼ minutes
Part II	5¼ minutes
Part III	4 minutes
Part IV	7¼ minutes
Total Performance Time	23¾ minutes

II. SPECIFIC CONSIDERATIONS

The Formal Scheme

William Grant Still defends the somewhat unorthodox form that is employed in the *Afro-American Symphony* in the following statement:

> When judged by the laws of musical form the *Symphony* is somewhat irregular. This irregularity is in my estimation justified since it has no ill effect on the proportional balance of the composition. Moreover, when one considers that an architect is free to design new forms of buildings, and bears in mind the freedom permitted creators in other fields of art, he can hardly deny a composer the privilege of altering established forms as long as the sense of proportion is justified.[7]

In the compositional philosophy of Mr. Still, melody has the position of foremost concern; however, he feels that melody must be supported and intensified by the use of a formal scheme that is logical, balanced, and clear. Form is the next most important element of composition. In a speech given for a Composer's Workshop in 1967, Mr. Still comments further on the importance of form:

> Once having decided upon which themes to use, I then go on to planning the form of the new composition. My usual practice is to map out a plan which conforms loosely to the established rules of musical form, and then to deviate from it as I see fit. This method serves as a stimulant to invention and inspiration.[8]

---

[7] Arvey, *op. cit.*, p. 24.

[8] Speech to Composer's Workshop, annual convention of National Association of Negro Musicians, Los Angeles, Calif., August 17, 1967.

FIRST MOVEMENT: MODERATO ASSAI

Outline of Form: First Movement

In Figures 1A to 1E following, the formal structure of the First Movement is presented in outline form. It is of interest to note that the rehearsal numbers assigned by the composer are placed to correspond with the sectional breakdown.

Figure 1A. Outline of Form — *Afro-American Symphony*: First Movement

NO.	PAGES	SECTION	NO. OF MEASURES	KEY	TEMPO	COMMENTS
1	5-6	INTRODUCTION	6	A FLAT MAJOR	♩=88	*Moderato assai;* mezzo-forte; common time; English horn solo in a rubato style; melody derived from the principal theme.
2	6-8	PRINCIPAL THEME *Blues* Theme (First subject)	12	SAME	SAME	Follows the pattern of the "standard" twelve-measure *Blues;* may be termed a multi-phrase period; consists of 3 four-measure units: 1. Statement of theme, 2. Imitation at the 2nd, 3. Imitation at the 5th, Melody in muted trumpet (Harmon mute); Contrapuntal texture.
3	8-11	RESTATEMENT OF *Blues* Theme	14	SAME	SAME	Clarinet on melody with contrapuntal texture in woodwinds; chordal texture in spiccato style; contains a 2-measure extension.

15

Figure 1B. Outline of Form — *Afro-American Symphony*: First Movement

NO.	PAGES	SECTION	NO. OF MEASURES	KEY	TEMPO	COMMENTS
4	11-13	VARIATION OF PRIN. THEME (Rhythmic)	12	A FLAT MAJOR	♩ =112	*piu mosso* Rhythmic variation of the *Blues* theme carried in the violins against a rhythmic counterpoint in the woodwinds/horns. Thesis—4 measures Antithesis—4 measures Transition—4 measures
5	13.14	SUBORDINATE THEME (Second subject)	8	G MAJOR	♩ =72	*andante cantabile* Second subject carried in the oboe; descant by the flute; counterpoint in low strings; plus arpeggiation in the harp. Multiple-textures. Masterful orchestration. Note the change to an unrelated key center: a nuance in 1930. Passage consists of a statement and a counter-statement both four measures in length.

Figure 1C. Outline of Form — *Afro-American Symphony*: First Movement

NO.	PAGES	SECTION	NO. OF MEASURES	KEY	TEMPO	COMMENTS
6	14-16	ALTERATION OF SUBORDINATE THEME	8	G		Slightly faster than 72, *poco piu mosso*; the subordinate theme is restated with a slight rhythmic alteration by the first violins, then by the flute.
7	16-17	VARIATION OF SUBORDINATE THEME	7	SAME	SAME	Melody in celli. (4 Ms.) Melody in harp. (4 Ms.) Note special harp effects, "with nails close to sounding board."
8	17-18	TRANSITIONAL PASSAGE	6	G MINOR		*Piu mosso Accelerando poco a poco sin al allegro.* Transitional passage in the strings building up to division two, (Development); thin texture mainly chordal; ends in an E 7 chord in the horns which prepares the new key, Ab minor.

16

Figure 1D. Outline of Form — *Afro-American Symphony*: First Movement

NO.	PAGES	SECTION	NO. OF MEASURES	KEY	TEMPO	COMMENTS
9	18-21	DIVISION II (DEVELOPMENT)	16	A FLAT MINOR	♩=160	*Allegro* Development of material from the principle theme, "Give-and-take" texture. Melodic line shifts from section to section every few measures.
10	21-23	CONTINUATION OF ABOVE	14	SAME	SAME	Richly orchestrated; much rhythmic counterpoint. First use of full orchestra.
11	24-25	DIVISION III (RECAPITULATION)	10	A FLAT MINOR	♩=72	*Andante cantabile* Subordinate theme now appears in Ab minor: a radical departure. Melody in violins, ctpt. in low strings; complex texture used, both contrapuntal and chordal at once; solos by bass clarinet and bassoons on extensions of the theme.

Figure 1E. Outline of Form — *Afro-American Symphony*: First Movement

NO.	PAGES	SECTION	NO. OF MEASURES	KEY	TEMPO	COMMENTS
12	25	TRANSITION	2	SAME	♩=88	*Tempo primo* A two-measure transitional passage, prepares new key (Ab major) and new, slower tempo.
12	26-28	RESTATEMENT OF PRINCIPAL THEME	14	A FLAT MAJOR	SAME	Final appearance of the principal theme, chordal texture, melody in the muted trumpet, rhythmic counterpoint in woodwinds, return to the strict *Blues* harmonic pattern: I, I7, IV, V7, I.
13	28-29	CODA	7	SAME	Slower	*Meno* Bass clarinet imitates the principal theme; complex harmony resolves to a "I6" chord: a prelude to modern, popular harmonic cliche. End of first movement. Total measures = 136. Time—7¼ minutes.

17

Thematic Material. Introductory Theme

The introduction to the First Movement of *Afro-American Symphony* is derived from the principal theme of that movement. The five-note melodic pattern shown under the bracket is taken directly from the first subject, note for note; the only change that occurs is in the rhythmic pattern. See Figures 2 and 3.

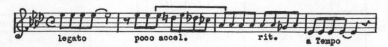

Figure 2. Introductory Theme: First Movement

The melody above is presented as a solo by the English horn—a favorite solo instrument of Mr. Still. The metronome marking for the introduction is eighty-eight for the quarter note. The plaintive sound of this solo creates a musical gesture which helps to reinforce the mood of the first movement—longing. The movement is prefaced by the following verse by Paul Laurence Dunbar which tends to enhance the extra-musical associations:

"All my life long twell de night has pas'
Let de wo'k come ez it will,
So dat I fin' you, my honey, at last',
Somewhaih des ovah de hill."[9]

The principal theme. Figure 3 below states the principal theme of the First Movement; the theme is also referred to as the first subject, but more often is described as the *Blues* theme.

Figure 3. Principal Theme (*Blues* theme)

---

[9] *The Life and Works of Paul Laurence Dunbar*, Dodd-Mead & Co., 1907 ed.

It is important to note that this theme adheres to the standard twelve-measure *Blues pattern*. Despite the fact that it is a typical *Blues* melody, it was not borrowed from existing folk music, but was a pure musical creation of the composer. Through the use of thematic transformation, variations of this theme are heard throughout the composition. These variations are musical gestures which serve as the factor of unification for the *Afro-American Symphony*.

Variation of Blues theme. Figure 4 below gives an example of Mr. Still's style of thematic transformation. The principal theme is repeated with certain alterations in the rhythmic and orchestral treatment.

Figure 4. Variation of the Blues Theme

Extended transition. An extended transitional passage occurs next. Figure 5 below shows yet another transformation of the *Blues* theme which is used in the transition. This is the fourth consecutive presentation of the principal theme. This transition leads to the subordinate theme.

Figure 5. Transition: Variation of *Blues* Theme

The subordinate theme. The composer describes the second subject as follows: "The Subordinate Theme in G Major is in the style of a Negro Spiritual and bears sort of a relationship to the *Blues* theme. The three-part song form is used here as follows: two measures of thesis, two measures of antithesis, and two measures of repetition of thesis." [10] Figures 6, 7, and 8 present the three elements of the subordinate theme.

---

10 William Grant Still, Speech to Composer's Workshop, 1967.

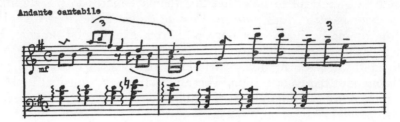

Figure 6. Subordinate Theme: Thesis

Figure 7. Subordinate Theme: Antithesis

Figure 8. Restatement of Thesis

The development. After a short treatment of the subordinate theme, a transitional section leads to the development, or Division Two as it is listed in Verna Arvey's booklet. Figure 9 states the opening phrase of the development section; this melody is derived from the *Blues* theme.

Figure 9. Development: Opening Theme

20

The Recapitulation. To use Mr. Still's words:

> Division three is a Recapitulation, in which there is a radical departure. The subordinate theme reappears in A flat minor, instead of a repetition of the principal theme.[11]
> The music rises to a climax and then diminishes as it nears the recapitulation.[12]

The motive of the recapitulation is seen in Figure 10 on the following page.

Figure 10. Recapitulation: Opening Theme

Harmonic Style Employed

Basically, the harmonies employed in the First Movement are relatively simple; the chords are largely dictated by the melodies. However, within this framework of simplicity, the composer devises harmonic nuance and variety.

Basic harmonic progression. The basic harmonic progression of the First Movement is the standard Blues progression: I, I^7, IV, V^7, I. The composer strays from this pattern many times, but the dominant-tonic relationship is always kept intact.

A prominent feature of *Blues* harmony is the tendency to move from the tonic toward the subdominant side of the key; in most cases the tonic seventh is used rather than the simple tonic triad. This I^7 to IV progression strongly resembles the V^7 to I relationship, but we do not actually feel that a modulation has occurred. Mr. Still occasionally uses a plagal relationship (IV to I), but there is a preponderance of the I^7 to IV and V^7 to I relationships in this movement.

[11] Verna Arvey, *op. cit.*, p. 25.
[12] W. G. Still, Speech to Composer's Workshop, 1967.

Use of the embellished triad. In the First Movement, the embellished triad occurs roughly twice as frequently as does the simple triad; the four-note chord far outnumbers all other chords. The most frequently used chord is the triad (major or minor) with the added minor seventh. The use of the added major seventh is rare in this entire symphony. The added ninth is used frequently with the dominant chord and occasionally with the subdominant. The triad with added sixth is used sparingly.

Tonic seventh as chord of repose. An interesting harmonic device is Mr. Still's use of the tonic seventh chord as a chord of repose. In many instances the I^7 does not move to the IV chord, but merely acts as an embellished I chord. This is an harmonic nuance and suggests the use of this device (quite possibly by accident) by jazz bands that traveled the Mississippi River in earlier years. In the jazz idiom, the added-seventh chord used as a chord of repose was used prior to the chord with added sixth.[13]

Tonic chord with added sixth. The final chord of the First Movement is a tonic chord with added sixth. This device had been used by earlier classical composers, especially in the late Romantic Period, but in 1930 the device was relatively new and fresh and added harmonic interest. Unfortunately, in the two decades that followed, this style of chord was grossly overused and became trite. Still's use of the chord, however, was in good taste and served, in a way, as a preview of things to come.

Texture of the orchestration. Four styles of texture are used by the composer; these styles may be referred to as chordal, contrapuntal, homophonic, and "give-and-take." The First Movement is multi-textured; however, the give-and-take texture predominates. Chordal texture is not used alone, but in conjunction with one of the other texture styles. Through the careful use of voicings and balance, Mr. Still is able to use dissonances that would normally be considered quite harsh, without creating a high degree of tension. The composer uses harsh dissonances, but they are softened through clever orchestration devices. Mr. Still looks upon dissonance as a "spice" that should be carefully mixed in, but certainly not overdone.[14]

---

[13] Gunther Schuller, *Early Jazz: Its Roots and Musical Development* (New York: Oxford University Press, 1968), pp. 38-43.

[14] Personal interview: Slattery-Still, 12 Feb. 1969.

Rhythmic considerations. The rhythmic patterns employed in the First Movement are basically simple; duple meter is used throughout the movement. In keeping with the traditions of the *Blues* idiom, the rhythmic style is characterized by the free and extensive use of syncopation. The *Blues* theme employs syncopation and the melodic use of the *blue* note. These two devices combine to form the basic musical gesture used to unite the entire symphony. Rhythmic alterations play an important role in Mr. Still's technique of thematic transformation.

It is important to note that the composer did not want the dotted eighth followed by the sixteenth note to be played in strict time. Explicit instructions are given on the score that the unit of beat should be thought of as being divided into three parts rather than into four. The above rhythmic figure should be mentally pictured as a quarter note and an eighth placed under a triplet ligature.[15] This is another example of the composer being true to the *Blues* idiom. This bastard form of beat division is an integral part of the *Blues*, jazz, and American popular music in general; it is autochthonous to American music.

SECOND MOVEMENT: ADAGIO

The Second Movement of the *Afro-American Symphony* is entitled *Adagio*. It is written in common time with a metronome marking of sixty-three for the quarter note. The key center is F (major or minor) throughout. The underlying mood reflected is that of sorrow[16] The movement is prefaced by the following excerpt by Paul Laurence Dunbar:

> "It's moughty tiahsome layin' 'roun'
> Dis sorrer-laden earfly groun'
> An' oftentimes I thinks, thinks I
> 'Twould be a sweet t'ing des to die
> An' go 'long home."

---

15 William Grant Still, *Afro-American Symphony* (New York: J. Fischer and Brother, 1935), p. 26.
16 Verna Arvey, *op. cit.,* p. 24.

Outline of Form: Second Movement

An outline of the form of the Second Movement along with pertinent comments is given on the following pages in Figures 11A, 11B, and 11C.

Figure 11A.   Outline of Form — *Afro-American Symphony*: Second Movement

NO.	PAGES	SECTION	NO. OF MEASURES	KEY	TEMPO	COMMENTS
14	30	INTRODUCTION	6	F	$\quad$=63	Solo violin on melody; chordal accompaniment in strings plus muffled tympani. Melody derived from last half of the 2nd measure of the *Blues* theme.
15	30-31	PRINCIPAL THEME	8	F	SAME	*Doloroso*: melody in the oboe with obligato by flute (contrapuntal); chordal accp. by strings; multi-textured; *Blue* note used as a grace note.
16	31-32	RESTATEMENT OF PRINCIPAL THEME	8	F Major and Minor	SAME	*Doloroso*; viola section on melody; . countermelody in flutes, clarinets and muted trumpets (Harmon mutes); *Blue* grace note appears in flute countermelody.
—	32	EXTENSION	1	SAME	*poco riten.*	A miniature codetta; helps to prepare the forthcoming transition.

24

Figure 11B. Outline of Form — *Afro-American Symphony*: Second Movement

NO.	PAGES	SECTION	NO. OF MEASURES	KEY	TEMPO	COMMENTS
16	32-33	TRANSITION	4	F	*rit.* *poco a poco*	Transition section; English horn solo set against chordal accomp. in strings; solo derived from intro. to 2nd mvmt.
17	33	SUBORDINATE THEME	4	F Major and Minor	*a tempo* M.M. 63	Melody starts in the fl. & continued in 1st vln. Melody derived from the *Blues* theme (1st mvmt.)
—	34	RESTATEMENT OF SUBORD. THEME	4	F	SAME	Melody in solo clarinet; chordal accompaniment by muted trombones. (Harmon mutes)
18	34-35	DEVELOPMENT OF PRIN. THEME	6	SAME	*piu mosso non tanto*	Rhythmic alteration of prin. theme; melody in 1st violin; chordal accp. in strings; ends with harp arpeggios and a *fermata*.
—	35-36	DEVELOPMENT (CONT.)	6	SAME	*poco piu mosso*	Melody in first violin four measures; melody in bass clarinet for two measure extension.

Figure 11C. Outline of Form — *Afro-American Symphony*: Second Movement

NO.	PAGES	SECTION	NO. OF MEASURES	KEY	TEMPO	COMMENTS
19	36-37	DEVELOPMENT (CONT.)	8	F Minor	*a tempo* M.M. 63	A continuation of the development of the principal theme; melodic line is passed around; some use of the full orchestra.
—	38	EXTENSION	2	SAME	*ritard.* *poco a poco*	Transition leads back to the principal theme; melody in the st. bass.
20	38-39	FINAL STATEMENT PRIN. THEME	9	F Major and Minor	*a tempo*	*Doloroso;* melody shared by flute and bassoon; chordal accompaniment in harp and low strings; counterpoint in violins; ritard and fermata.
21	39	CODA	8	F	M.M. 63	Introductory motive restated by 1st violin over a contrapuntal then chordal accmp. by strings. Ends on a simple triad; constantly diminishing to *il piu piano possible.* Total performance time is 5¼ minutes.

25

Thematic Material: Second Movement

The principal theme. The principal theme of the Second Movement is first stated by the solo oboe accompanied by violas and *'celli divisi* and by a flute obligato. This theme is stated in Figure 12 below.

Figure 12. Principal Theme: Second Movement

The subordinate theme. The subordinate theme of the Second Movement is an alteration of the *Blues* theme. In its initial presentation, the theme is given to the flute. Theme is depicted in Figure 13 below.

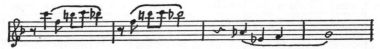

Figure 13. Subordinate Theme: Second Movement

Alteration of principal theme. The section that follows the subordinate theme is described by Mr. Still: "Then comes an alteration of the principal theme of the Second Movement that represents the fervent prayers of a burdened people rising upward to God." [17] The rising of the prayers to God is depicted musically by ascending *arpeggios* on the harp. [18] In his speech to the Composer's Workshop in 1967, the composer further stated: "Finally, a variation of the *Blues* theme, followed by a return to the principal theme of the Second Movement leads to a coda built on the

---

[17] Speech to Composer's Workshop, 1967.
[18] *Afro-American Symphony,* p. 34.

26

same material as that of the Introduction to this movement." The above-mentioned variation of the *Blues* theme is stated in Figure 14 below.

Figure 14. Variation of *Blues* Theme

Important Features of Second Movement

Harmonic considerations. The harmonic vocabulary of the Second Movement is more complex than that of the First Movement; there is an extensive use of chords of addition and chords of omission. Altered chords based on scale degrees II, IV, V, and VII are plentiful; on two occasions altered III and VI chords are introduced. Some of the alterations that may occur in a given chord are:

1. Raising or lowering the root
2. Raising or lowering the fifth
3. Flatting the ninth
4. Raising the seventh

The above alterations occur in an infinite variety of combinations. Other colorful chords that appear in this movement are:

1. Triad with added major seventh
2. Diminished triad
3. Augmented triad (usually with seventh)
4. Diminished seventh chord
5. Chords with added sixth
6. Chords containing both the major and minor third

The harmonic speed is moderate; there is rarely more than one chord change per measure. The standard *Blues* progression is not utilized in this movement. The plagal mode (I, IV, I) using complex alterations is given much usage. The modified dominant is the preponderant harmonic device used in this movement. Points of departure and arrival are clear and well defined; this feature is accomplished through the careful handling of the melodic line in conjunction with the harmonic structure.

27

Texture. The texture of the Second Movement is basically homophonic. The last five measures of the coda display a purely chordal texture. As in the First Movement, normally harsh dissonances are softened through careful voicing of the chords and through a delicate balance in the orchestration.

Rhythmic considerations. The rhythmic figures are simple, direct, and held in bounds by the bar lines. The use of syncopation is again much in evidence.

Unification factor. By means of masterful thematic transformation, elements of the *Blues* theme are presented in the introduction and in the subordinate theme. A variation of the *Blues* theme also occurs after the subordinate theme. These musical gestures serve as a strong factor of unification throughout the composition.

Element of pathos. The sob and the sigh are vocal gestures that may suggest sorrow, frustration, or despair. In the Second Movement, these vocal gestures are imitated by the composer through the use of melodic nuance. The half steps and the "blue notes" used as grace notes in the melodic line strongly suggest the slight vocal inflection involved in the sigh or the sob. The listener is led toward this type of interpretation by the title of the movement, *Sorrow,* and by the verse of Dunbar which is used as a Preface.

The combination of the title, the verse, and the imitation of vocal gestures can readily bring about a strong spiritual enactment on the part of the listener and the performer. Probably the most important feature of the Second Movement is the powerful element of pathos involved therein.

THIRD MOVEMENT: *ANIMATO*

The Third Movement of the *Afro-American Symphony* is entitled *Animato.* It is written in common time with a metronome marking of 116 for the quarter note. The key center is A flat (major and minor) throughout. The underlying mood reflected is that of humor. The following verse by Paul Laurence Dunbar prefaces the movement:

> "An' we'll shout ouah halleluyahs,
> On dat mighty reck'nin' day."

Outline of Form: Third Movement

An outline of the form of the Third Movement along with pertinent comments is given on the following pages in Figures 15A, 15B, and 15C.

Figure 15A.   Outline of Form — *Afro-American Symphony*: Third Movement

NO.	PAGES	SECTION	NO. OF MEASURES	KEY	TEMPO	COMMENTS
22	40-41	INTRODUCTION	7	A FLAT	♩ =116	*Animato*; melodic material derived from prin. theme (1st subject). Melody in clarinet, bassoon, two horns, and 'cello.
23	41-42	PRINCIPAL THEME (FIRST SUBJECT)	8	SAME	SAME	Melody in strings; horns carry rhythmic ctrpt.; standard *Blues* progression used; thesis: four measures; antithesis: four measures; Banjo is used on afterbeats as a chordal accompaniment.
24	43-46	PRINCIPAL THEME (SECOND SUBJECT)	8	SAME	SAME	Woodwinds and violins on unison melody: brass on chordal accompaniment; thesis and antithesis form used again. Harmonic speed quickens: four chords per measure. Series of secondary dominants used for the first time . . . marked *tutta forza*.

29

Figure 15B. Outline of Form — *Afro-American Symphony*: Third Movement

NO.	PAGES	SECTION	NO. OF MEASURES	KEY	TEMPO	COMMENTS
25	44-46	RESTATEMENT OF PRIN. THEME (1st SUBJECT)	8	A FLAT	SAME (116)	Thesis (4 Ms.) oboe solo with rhythmic counterpoint in clarinet, harp and strings. Antithesis (4Ms): clarinet and flute on melody ending with bass clarinet solo. Give-and-take texture is predominant.
26	46-48	TRANSITION SECTION (THEME I)	7	A FLAT MINOR	SAME	Theme I is derived from 2nd subject (principal theme). Melody first in trombone then in unison with horn, woodwinds, viola and cello; then passes to 1st violin.
—	49	THEME II	8	SAME	SAME	Woodwinds and first violin on melody; rhythmic countermelody in trumpets and trombones.

Figure 15C. Outline of Form — *Afro-American Symphony*: Third Movement

NO.	PAGES	SECTION	NO. OF MEASURES	KEY	TEMPO	COMMENTS
27 & 28	49-52	DEVELOPMENT	22	A FLAT MAJOR	SAME (116)	Development of principal theme: first subject; marked *graziosamente*. Give-and-take texture is predominant; melodic line passes through fls., oboe and clars; strings; Eng. horn & bassoon; and finally trumpets, trombones, tuba, 'celli and string bass.
29	52-54	RECAPITULATION (1st SUBJECT)	8	SAME	SAME	Thesis and antithesis form used again; melody in woodwinds & strings; Banjo re-enters
30 —	54-55 56	RECAP. (2nd SUBJECT) EXTENSION	8 3	SAME	SAME	Thesis and antithesis; strings and woodwinds carry the melodic line.
31	56-58	CODA	13	SAME	SAME	Alteration of principal theme: (1st subject) in strings, piccolo, oboe and clarinet; *Blues* theme is played by trpt. and trbn.; full orchestra; richly textured; high tension.

Thematic Material: Third Movement.

The introduction. The introductory theme of the Third Movement of the *Afro-American Symphony* is presented in Figure 16 below. This melodic material is derived from the first subject of the principal theme.

Figure 16. Introduction: Third Movement

The principal theme. The introductory material is followed by the principal theme, first subject. This first subject is divided into a thesis and an antithesis. This pattern of thesis and antithesis is used throughout the Third Movement. The thesis of the first subject is stated in Figure 17 below; the thesis of the second subject is shown in Figure 18 on the following page.

Figure 17. Principal Theme: First Subject

31

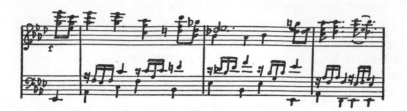

Figure 18. Principal Theme: Second Subject

Variation of first subject. Following the statement of the second subject, the first subject is repeated in a slightly different form. This variation is seen in Figure 19 below.

Figure 19. Variation of First Subject

Figure 20. Transition Section: Theme I

Transitional themes. The transitional material is divided into Themes I and II. Figure 20 above presents Theme I which is derived from the second subject of the principal theme. Theme II is introduced by the woodwinds and the first violins while the trum-

32

pets and trombones play a countermelody. Theme II is stated in Figure 21 below.

Figure 21. Transitional Section: Theme II

The development. The development section elaborates on the thematic material of the first subject of the principal theme. Figures 22 and 23 demonstrate the orchestration technique of William Grant Still.

Figure 22. Development of First Subject: Principal Theme

33

Figure 23. Continuation of Development

The recapitulation. Figure 24 presents the recapitulation of the first subject of the principal theme.

Figure 24. Recapitulation of First Subject

The coda. Figure 25 on the following page presents the first four measures from the closing passage of the Third Movement. The upper score displays an alteration of the first subject of the principal theme carried by piccolo, oboe, clarinet and strings. The lower score shows a restatement of the *Blues* theme from the First Movement taken by trumpets and trombones.

34

Figure 25. The Coda

Important Features of the Third Movement

Harmonic considerations. The points of arrival and departure are again clearly marked by the harmonic progressions. The standard *Blues* progression is frequently used.

The composer uses a series of secondary dominants for the first time in this composition; this series runs: I, VI⁷, II⁷, V⁷, I (see page 43 of score). This device has been referred to as a "Barbershop progression." In later years this progression became a standard jazz effect.

Other points of harmonic interest are:
1. First use of II^7, III, VI, and VI^7 chords
2. Extended use of tonic with added sixth
3. First use of chord with added fourth (this is actually an added eleventh). (page 47 of score)
4. Continued use of major/minor sonorities
5. Continued use of chords of addition and chords of omission
6. Use of unusual chord: root plus major third plus two superimposed tritones (see page 48 of score)

The harmonic speed is moderate until the last section. From page fifty-four onward (the final twenty-four measures), the harmonic speed increases greatly with four separate chords per measure. This results in a heightening of tension which carries through to the end of the movement.

Although some complex sonorities are used for purposes of coloration, the basic harmonic progressions remain relatively simple. Only tertial sonorities are used in this movement and throughout the entire composition.

Rhythmic considerations. A steady, brisk tempo is maintained throughout the movement. This contributes to the "happy-go-lucky" mood that the composer wishes to reflect.

The Scherzo is characterized by the use of two rhythmic motives which are utilized in almost every section. The rhythmic motives are:

These motives serve as a unifying factor for the entire movement.

Texture. "Give-and-take" texture is predominant throughout most of the Scherzo. The coda section, however, is multi-textured, containing a combination of contrapuntal and homophonic styles.

Other features. The tenor banjo is used in this movement to accentuate the strong, dance-like rhythms. The cheerful "twang" of this instrument on the chordal afterbeat suggests the occasional fun session of the southern Negro of earlier years; one can readily picture a plantation party or a Saturday night dance. There is a strong possibility that this is the first use of the banjo in a composition of symphonic magnitude.

The Scherzo, as the Third Movement is commonly referred to, won immediate and enthusiastic response from the audiences. For a period of time it stood out as a separate entity from the rest of the composition. This is demonstrated by the fact that the first recordings were made of the Scherzo only. Howard Hanson directed for a Victor recording and Leopold Stokowski conducted for a Columbia recording, neither of which is available commercially at this time.

Verna Arvey comments on the first Berlin performance of the *Afro-American Symphony* in 1933:

> An audience in Berlin broke a twenty-year tradition to encore the Scherzo from this Symphony when Dr. Howard Hanson conducted it there; several years later, when Karl Krueger conducted it in Budapest, his audience did the same thing.[19]

[19] Arvey, *op. cit.*, p. 23.

FOURTH MOVEMENT: LENTO, CON RISOLUZIONE

The Fourth Movement of the *Afro-American Symphony* is en-titled *Lento, con risoluzione*. The movement opens in three quarter time with a metronome marking of sixty-six for the quarter note; the opening key center is E major. However, both the tempo and the key center are altered frequently. The suggestive title given to this movement is *Sincerity*.[20] The movement is prefaced by the following poetic excerpt by Paul Laurence Dunbar:

"Be proud, my Race, in mind and soul.
Thy name is writ on Glory's scroll
In characters of fire.
High mid the clouds of Fame's bright sky
Thy banner's blazoned folds now fly,
And truth shall lift them higher."

Outline of the Form: Fourth Movement

An outline of the form of the Fourth Movement along with pertinent comments is given on the following pages in Figures 26A, 26B, and 26C.

Figure 26A. Outline of Form — *Afro-American Symphony*: Fourth Movement

NO.	PAGES	SECTION	NO. OF MEASURES	KEY	TEMPO	COMMENTS
32	59	PRINCIPAL THEME	16	E MAJOR	♩=66	Thesis and antithesis: 8 meas. each; melody in violins, violas, and 'c e l l i; countermelody in string bass and bass clarinet.
33	60	PRIN. THEME (ALTERED AND EXTENDED)	12	SAME	SAME	Strings same as above; woodwinds and brass play a chordal accompaniment..
34	61	SUBORDINATE THEME	4	A MAJOR	♩=88	*Piu mosso*; three-measure theme plus one measure extension; soli by oboe and flute with chordal accomp. in strings; material derived f r o m *Blues* theme (1st mvmt.)
—	62	RESTATEMENT (SUBORDINATE THEME)	4	C MAJOR	SAME	Flute and clarinet soli; strings on chordal accompaniment.
35	62-63	VARIATION (SUBORDINATE THEME)	10	F MAJOR	SAME	Thesis: 4 meas.; antithesis: 4 meas.; plus a 2 - measure extension Melody passed around; English horn, solo in the extension *(piu lento)*; multi-textured.

20 *Ibid.*, p. 24.

Figure 26B.　Outline of Form — *Afro-American Symphony*: Fourth Movement

NO.	PAGES	SECTION	NO. OF MEASURES	KEY	TEMPO	COMMENTS
36	63-64	DEVELOPMENT SUBORDINATE THEME	14	F MAJOR	♩=112	Oboe, clarinet and first violin on unisonal melody; multi - textured background; melody passes to flutes then to woodwinds, horns and trumpets.
37	65-67	DEVELOPMENT SUBORDINATE THEME	28	F MINOR	♩=72	*Andante, molto expressivo;* Section o p e n s with a m e l o d y in strings; obligato for bassoon. Melody in flute, flute and bassoon; then strings and woodwinds; *stringendo.*
38	66-67	(CONTINUA-TION)	—	—	—	
39	67	EXTENSION	3	—	—	
39	67-68	TRANSITION SECTION	8	NOT FIXED	SAME	Key center uncertain; modulatory passage; oboe solo with accompaniment in clarinet f a m i l y; chordal accompaniment. Complex harmonies.
40	68-69	VARIATION OF PRINCIPAL THEME	16	C SHARP MINOR	♩=66	*Lento, con risoluzione;* Soli in 'celli, *cantabile,* countermelody in flutes; melody next to 1st violin; homophonic texture; unusual chord progression (see harmonic coverage).

Figure 26C.　Outline of Form — *Afro-American Symphony*: Fourth Movement

NO.	PAGES	SECTION	NO. OF MEASURES	KEY	TEMPO	COMMENTS
41	69	VARIATION PRIN. THEME	8	E MAJOR	SAME 66	Melody in 'celli; harp carries countermelody; ends on III chord; G sharp minor.
42	70	TRANSITION INTRODUCTORY	6	NOT FIXED	♩=112	*Vivace;* 6/8 time; prepares for a scherzo-like r e s u m e of several themes; colorful chord progression.
43	71-73	VARIATION PRIN. THEME	16	A FLAT MAJOR	SAME	Extensive use of give-and-take texture; many complex sonorities.
44 TO 47	74-82	VARIATION PRIN. THEME	45	C MINOR	SAME	Mostly give - and - take texture; melody passed throughout orchestra; simpler sonorities now.
48	82-85	CLOSING THEME	17	F MINOR	♩=72	*Maestoso;* Brasses play a variation of principal theme, altered and extended; remainder of orchestra plays a continuous "multiple-ostinato." Continuous ostinato based on F minor chord; no ritard; full orchestra.
—	86-88	CODA	9	SAME	SAME	

Thematic Material: Fourth Movement

The principal theme. The principal theme of the Fourth Movement is initially stated by the strings with chordal accompaniment by clarinets, trombones, tuba, and string bass. The principal theme is presented in Figure 27 below.

Figure 27. Principal Theme: Fourth Movement

Figure 28. Subordinate Theme: Fourth Movement

The subordinate theme. The subordinate theme of the Fourth Movement is derived from the *Blues* theme of the First Movement. This is a further example of how the composer used the technique of thematic transformation as a factor of unification. The subordinate theme is shown in Figure 28.

Important Features of the Fourth Movement

Harmonic considerations. The sonorities of the Fourth Movement are the most complex of the entire composition. Mr. Still exhausts the possibilities of tertial sonority. There is a marked in-

39

crease in chords which contain both the major and the minor third. The chord of the diminished seventh is used frequently (see pages 64 and 65 of score). Despite the increase in complexity of the chords, there are sections where the harmonic speed is extremely slow.

The points of arrival are not as clear as they are in other movements; this is partially caused by the overlapping or extension of melodic figures into new sections. The standard *Blues* progression is not a significant factor in this movement.

Rhythmic considerations. The manner in which the composer handles the rhythmic variations in six-eight time is the most prominent rhythmic feature of this movement. The use of *ritardando* and *accelerando* is greatly increased.

The composer's description. In his speech to A Composer's Workshop in 1967, Mr. Still describes the Fourth Movement thus:

> The Fourth Movement is largely a retrospective viewing of the earlier movements with the exception of its principal theme. It is intended to give musical expression to the lines from Paul Laurence Dunbar which appear on the score: "Be proud, my race, in mind and soul . . ."

A summarization of the important features of *Afro-American Symphony* will be presented in the next section.

P. H. S.

A DISCUSSION OF THE *FOURTH SYMPHONY* INCLUDING COMPARISONS WITH THE *FIRST SYMPHONY*

The purpose of this chapter is twofold: (1) important background information on *Autochthonous* is presented along with an enumeration of the important features of this Symphony, and (2) a comparison of the pertinent features of *Autochthonous* and *Afro-American* is drawn. Comparisons are drawn with reference to the nine specific areas listed in the Introductory Note.

I.   GENERAL CONSIDERATIONS

The Creation of Autochthonous

The composer's intention. *Autochthonous* was not intended as a programmatic work. Mr. Still comments on this: "Both the *Afro-American* and the *Autochthonous* were similar in the sense that both were written as pure music—and a program, or descriptive notes, added after the completion of the music." [1] The composer further states: "The *Afro-American*, however, was intended to describe the American Negro from the outset, while *Autochthonous* was intended to be descriptive of the American spirit, as the subtitle implies." [2]

The compositional process. The composer has supplied the following detailed information concerning the actual writing of *Autochthonous:*

> I began the *Autochthonous* on July 22, 1947, decided to subtitle it "Autochthonous" on July 31st, and completed the sketch on September 4th. I had been composing (i.e., working on the sketch) steadily, and as soon as the sketch of a movement was completed, I had started to score it, going on to the composition of the next movement meanwhile. On September 8th, the entire Symphony was completed and I took the master sheets to the blueprint company, after which I started to extract the parts and to proofread what I had already done. [3]

The addition of program notes. The program notes that were devised by Mr. and Mrs. Still read as follows:

---

[1] Slattery-Still correspondence, April 25, 1969.
[2] *Ibid.*
[3] *Ibid.*

41

The Autochthonous was written in Los Angeles, in the house where we lived for twenty years, and where our children were born: 3670 Cimarron Street. The Symphony was copyrighted October 20, 1947.[4]

This Symphony, dedicated to the composer's old friend and teacher at Oberlin, Maurice Kessler, is subtitled "Autochthonous" to explain that the music has its roots in our own soil, and portrays—in a sense —the spirit of the American people. The First Movement exemplifies the feeling of optimism and energy: The American ability to "get things done." The Second Movement is more pensive, then, in the "second subject," animated in a folky way. The Third Movement is humorous and unmistakably typical of our country and its rhythms. The final movement depicts the warmth and the spiritual side of the American people—their love of mankind.

It may also be said that the music speaks of the fusion of musical cultures in North America.[5]

Significant Data

Brief descriptive statement. The *Fourth Symphony* is a multitextured, tonal composition in four movements. There is much emphasis placed upon the free flow of the melodic line. The form is generally free with a vague reference to traditional patterns. The harmonic vocabulary includes both tertial and nontertial sonorities. The points of departure and arrival are generally clear and well defined. Although two or more style idioms are used, the overall impression of the compositional style that is of Neoromanticism.

First performance. The *Fourth Symphony* was first performed in Oklahoma City on March 18, 1951. This performance was broadcast over the Mutual Radio Network with Victor Alessandro conducting the Oklahoma Symphony Orchestra.[6]

Instrumental requirements. Woodwinds: three flutes (third interchangeable with piccolo), two oboes, English horn, two clarinets in B flat, bass clarinet in B flat, and two bassoons (second interchangeable with contra bassoon).

Brass: four horns in F, three trumpets in B flat, three trombones, and one tuba.

Percussion: timpani, glockenspiel, resonator bell in G, triangle, wire brushes, small cymbal (suspended), large cymbal (sus-

---

4 The Still family lived at this address from 1939 until 1959. They then moved to their present location: 1262 Victoria Avenue, Los Angeles. The two children mentioned are Duncan and Judith.

5 Slattery-Still correspondence.

6 *Ibid.*

pended), cymbals, small snare drum, military drum, bass drum, and celesta.

Strings: normal string section plus the harp.

Time breakdown:

First Movement .... 7' 5"
Second Movement .... 7' 37"
Third Movement .... 3' 25"
Fourth Movement .... 10' 50"
Total Performance Time .... 28' 57"

II. SPECIFIC CONSIDERATIONS

FIRST MOVEMENT: MODERATELY

Synopsis of the Form

The form of the First Movement of *Autochthonous* is best described as "free." However, there is a suggested reference to *sonata allegro* form. The basic sections of the First Movement consist of an introduction, a statement of the principal theme with elaboration, and a statement of the second subject with elaboration. This is followed by series of alternating variations on the two main themes, ending in a short coda.

The pattern of key centers is as follows: D major, D minor, D major, C major, D minor, and D major. The basic tempo of the movement is 126 for the quarter note; this remains steady throughout. There are no *caesuras*. There is a short section where the metric pattern alternates between two-four and four-four time.

Thematic Material

The introduction. The introduction is stated by the bassoon, bass trombone, tuba, 'celli, and the string basses. The thematic material is derived from the second subject of this movement. The introductory motive is stated in Figure 29.

mf broadly
Figure 29. Introductory Theme: First Movement

43

The principal theme. The principal theme of the First Movement is initially stated by the strings in chordal texture. A counter-melody is heard first in the clarinet, then in the bassoon. This theme has a significant role in this composition; it acts as the factor of unification much the same as the *Blues* theme serves in the *Afro-American Symphony*. In various altered forms, this theme is used as the second subject of the next three Movements. The principal theme is presented in Figure 30.

Figure 30. Principal Theme: First Movement

The second subject. The second subject is introduced by the trumpets in chordal texture. The composer calls for mutes and supplies the following directions: "Preferably mutes with which a more delicate and less piercing tone may be obtained." [7] The *legato* chords of the trumpets are accompanied by *staccato* chords in the strings. The distant relationships of the chords involved, E flat major and G major, produces a polychordal effect. The poly-chordal sonorities are extended for a section of four measures.

The second subject of this Movement is presented in Figure 31.

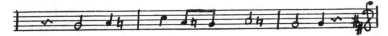

Figure 31. Second Subject: First Movement

Important Features of the First Movement

Harmonic considerations. In this Movement, there is an extended use of chords of addition. The most prominent added notes are the major second, sixth, seventh, and ninth scale degrees. A moderately harsh dissonance is created by the use of "cluster" chords. These "cluster" chords are formed by placing the root, major second, and major or minor third in a closed position; this produces a reasonably high degree of tension. Quartal-quintal chords and tritone chords are used in juxtaposition with tertial sonorities.

---

[7] Score of *Autochthonous Symphony*, No. 4, p. 4.

Polychordal sonorities are used to some degree, but these sections are of short duration. The harmonic speed of the Movement is relatively fast. The points of arrival and departure are clear and well defined. The overall harmonic style moves away from Neoromanticism in the direction of Modernism.

Texture. The First Movement contains a wide variety of textural styles ranging from unisons to polychordality. Chordal and "give-and-take" styles are the most prominent.

Rhythmic considerations. Except for a short section of alternating two-four and four-four measures, the basic meter is kept intact. The meter is held within bounds by the bar lines. The use of syncopation is prominent.

Comparison with First Movement of Afro-American

Areas of similarity. The First Movements of the *Afro-American* and *Autochthonous* are similar in the following areas:

1. Formal structure
2. Use of thematic transformation
3. Factors of unification
4. Orchestration technique
5. Limited rhythmic complexity
6. Strong emphasis on a tonal center

Areas of contrast. The greatest area of contrast is found in the harmonic vocabulary employed. The vocabulary of the *Afro-American* is basically limited to tertial sonorities with added-tone chords. The sonorities used in *Autochthonous* are much more complex, involving quartal-quintal chords, tritone chords, and polychordality. The use of an extended harmonic vocabulary enlarges the possibilities for creating higher levels of tension and for attaining a greater variety of expression. The basic style of the *Afro-American* is Neoromantic, while the First Movement of *Autochthonous* leans more toward the Modern idiom. A summarization of the areas of similarity and of contrast will be given at the end of this chapter.

45

SECOND MOVEMENT: SLOWLY

Thematic Material

The introduction. The introduction to the Second Movement is derived from the principal theme of the First Movement. The opening melody is stated by the flute with chordal accompaniment by the woodwinds; it is then repeated by the string section. The introduction to the Second Movement is presented in Figure 32.[8]

Figure 32. Introduction: Second Movement

The principal theme. The principal theme of the Second Movement is first stated as an oboe solo with a contrapuntal accompaniment first in the violas and 'celli and then in the horns.[9] This theme is seen in Figure 33.

Figure 33. Principal Theme: Second Movement

The second subject. The second subject is a variation of the principal theme of the First Movement. The melody is carried by the first violins with a chordal accompaniment by the other strings.[10] Figure 34 shows the second subject.

Figure 34. Second Subject: Second Movement

---

[8] Score of Autochthonous Symphony, No. 19, p. 24.

[9] *Ibid.*, No. 20, p. 24.

[10] *Ibid.*, No. 23, p. 28.

Important Features of the Second Movement

The Second Movement is characterized by vivid contrasts in dynamics, texture, tempo, and the level of tension. The harmonic vocabulary includes chords with the highest level of tension that is possible to attain such as tritone sonorities and chords with an added minor second, major seventh, or minor ninth. Other highly dissonant chords the composer used are chords which contain both the major and the minor third, or both the major and the minor seventh, and chords that contain both the augmented and the diminished fifth. On the other hand, the vocabulary also includes unisons which are placed at the other end of the tension cycle.

The form of the Second Movement bears a vague relationship to *sonata allegro* form. Points of departure and of arrival are well defined and correspond with the changes in the tension-release cycle This cycle is accomplished mainly through harmonic means. The principal building device of this Movement is thematic transformation, which also serves as the factor of unification.

Comparison with Second Movement of Afro-American

Areas of similarity. The strongest point of similarity between the Second Movements of the two Symphonies is the element of pathos involved. The six areas of similarity listed above for the First Movements apply to the Second Movements also.

Areas of contrast. The Second Movement of *Autochthonous* uses more dissonances and the dissonances are more extreme in terms of producing harmonic tension. As a result, the tension-release cycle has a wider range. In general, the contrasts are more vivid than in the Second Movement of the *Afro-American Symphony*.

THIRD MOVEMENT: MODERATELY FAST

Thematic Material

The principal theme. The principal theme of the Third Movement is presented by flutes and oboe in octaves. The cello section provides a "walking bass" accompaniment. This theme is presented in Figure 35.

47

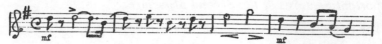

Figure 35. Principal Theme: Third Movement

The principal theme is preceded by a humorous introduction stated by a clarinet and a bassoon accompanied by wire brushes on a military drum.[11]

The second subject. After a series of variations which alternate between the principal theme and the introductory material, the second subject is presented by three flutes in chordal texture. A contrapuntal accompaniment appears in the clarinet and bassoons.[12] The second subject is presented in Figure 36. It is derived from the principal theme of the First Movement; this is another example of the process of unification.

Figure 36. Second Subject: Third Movement

Important Features of the Third Movement

Harmonic considerations. The extent of the harmonic vocabulary is greatly reduced in this movement; the chords are basically less complex. As a result, the range of the tension-release cycle is not as extreme as it was in the First and Second Movements. The harmonic speed is relatively slow. The harmonic progressions are similar to those used in the popular style of the 1940's known as "boogie-woogie." Much use is made of the "walking bass," an ostinato which outlines the chord. Extensive use is made of the triad with added sixth.

Rhythmic considerations. The pulse remains steady throughout at a tempo of 104 for the quarter note. Extensive use is made of the dotted eighth followed by a sixteenth rhythmic figure. Syncopated figures are also abundant.

Texture. The texture is mostly "give-and-take." Certain sections, however, imitate the chordal texture of the "big band sound" of the 1940's. The melodic lead is passed around to a wide variety

---

11 Score of *Autochthonous*, No. 29, p. 34.
12 *Ibid.*, No. 35, p. 40.

of instruments, each solo instrument retaining the melody for just a few measures.

The general feeling suggested by this Movement is one of gaiety. The melodic line is playful and witty. The mood is one of Americans in a carefree frame of mind, perhaps attending a dance.

Similarity to the Scherzo of Afro-American. As he does in the Scherzo of the First Symphony, Mr. Still again takes a large step away from the cliches of traditional symphonic compositions by introducing strikingly new elements into his Scherzos. Both of these Scherzos are witty, carefree, humorous, and dancelike in nature; both are basically simple.

FOURTH MOVEMENT: SLOWLY AND REVERENTLY

Thematic Material

The principal theme. The principal theme of the Fourth Movement is initially stated by the first violins. The other strings and the bassoons provide a chordal accompaniment.[13] The principal theme is shown in Figure 37.

Figure 37. Principal Theme: Fourth Movement

Episodic material. The Fourth Movement is composed in one of the higher Rondo forms. The principal theme alternates with an episode derived from the principal theme of the First Movement and with an episode based on the principal theme of this Movement.[14] The latter is shown in Figure 38.

Figure 38. Episodic Material: Fourth Movement

13 *Ibid.,* No. 42, p. 50.
14 *Ibid.,* No. 43, p. 50.

Important Features of the Fourth Movement

Harmonic considerations. Harsh dissonances are used in abundance, but their "biting" effect is softened somewhat by clever orchestration technique. The most severe dissonances are obtained by the use of added tones, polychordality, and major/minor sonorities. Frequently used added tones are the major second and the major seventh. The limits of the tension-release cycle are not as extreme as in the First and Second Movements. The harmonic speed varies between moderately fast and moderately slow. The triad with added sixth is used extensively and is treated as a chord of repose.

Texture. The Fourth Movement is multi-textured; a wide range of textural schemes is employed. Much emphasis is placed on chordal texture with the separate sections of the orchestra being used as blocks of tone color. The prominent textural styles employed are chordal, polychordal, and "give-and-take." The Movement is characterized by frequent, vivid changes in tone color and texture. The masterful skill in the art of orchestration possessed by Mr. Still is fully demonstrated in this Movement.

Other features. The Fourth Movement is marked by frequent changes in the tonal center and the tempo. The level of tension builds moderately rapidly to a peak and then drops off instantly. Free-flowing, *cantabile* melodies predominate.

Comparison with Fourth Movement of Afro-American

Areas of similarity. The two Fourth Movements are similar in formal structure, the use of thematic transformation, the factors of unification, orchestration technique, limited rhythmic complexity, and strong tonal emphasis. The mood of each is meditative and reverent. The basic style of composition is the same—Neoromantic.

Areas of contrast. The harmonic vocabulary of the *Autochthonous* Movement is more extensive than that of the *Afro-American* Movement. Accordingly, the tension-release cycle has a greater range of extremes. In the former, there are frequent changes in key, tempo, and texture; this is done to a greater degree than in the latter. The vividness of contrasts is more extreme in the *Autochthonous* Movement.

III.   SUMMARY OF COMPARISONS

The following comparisons are drawn with reference to the nine specific areas listed in the Introductory Note (p. 10).

Formal structure. The principals of formal structure are the same in both Symphonies. Mr. Still retains a limited reference to traditional forms, but alters and extends these forms to suit the needs of a given composition. The composer places his emphasis on balance, unity and variety of expression.

Harmonic structure and vocabulary. In the *Afro-American Symphony*, the harmonic structure is dictated mainly by the standard *Blues* progression. *Autochthonous* is not limited by any set progression except in the Third Movement where the chord progressions of popular music are followed loosely. Although there is an extensive use of modified dominant sonorities, the basic dominant-tonic relationship is kept intact in both compositions.

The harmonic vocabulary of the *First Symphony* is basically limited to tertial sonorities which is in keeping with the stated intent of the composition. The *Fourth Symphony* utilizes all of the harmonic devices of the *First Symphony* and goes beyond this to include tritone sonorities, quartel-quintal chords, and polytonality. Probably the most striking area of contrast between the two compositions is in the harmonic styles employed.

Origin of themes and thematic development. Mr. Still borrowed nothing from other composers or from folk music. All of the themes of both works are creations of the composer.

Mr. Still feels that the ability to develop and transform a theme is one of the most important assets that a composer should cultivate. His remarkable ability in this area is clearly manifested in both works. This is probably the strongest point of similarity between the two Symphonies.

Variety of expression. The methods that Mr. Still used to obtain variety of expression are much the same in both compositions. A listing of these devices could be quite extensive. A few of the more important devices are thematic transformation, melodic nuances, harmonic nuances, both subtle and abrupt changes in tone color, rhythmic variations, key changes, tempo changes, caesuras, and special instrumental effects.

Orchestration technique. The composer is a masterful orchestrator. This fact is amply manisfested in both works. In the first two movements of *Autochthonous,* there is little attempt made to soften the harshness of dissonances through orchestration technique.

Rhythmic devices employed. The composer remained rather on the conservative side in his use of rhythmic patterns and in the subdivision of the beat. The meter is always held within bounds by the barlines. Syncopation and dotted rhythms are used extensively in both compositions. Mr. Still avoided the highly complex subdivision of the beat that is prominent in much of the music of the Modern idiom. The rhythmic devices employed in both Symphonies are markedly similar. One slight area of contrast would be the 6/8 variation in the Fourth Movement of the *Afro-American.*

Tension-release cycle. The tension-release cycle of the two Symphonies is accomplished through the following means: (1) harmonic vocabulary, (2) harmonic speed, (3) level of dynamics, and (4) texture. The points of departure generally coincide with a low level of tension. The Points of arrival coincide with the *extremes* of the tension cycle. The main point of contrast is that *Autochthonous* contains extreme points of tension in comparison to those of the *Afro-American.*

Basic compositional style. The basic compositional style of the *Afro-American Symphony* is similar to the style of *Autochthonous.* The *Afro-American* remains basically in the *Blues* idiom. It may be termed a neoromantic composition. *Autochthonous* cannot be described as containing one basic style idiom; it is a combination of quasi-modern, popular, and neoromantic styles.

P. S.

SUMMARY

The following paragraphs summarize the comprehensive portrayal of William Grant Still:

Still's compositional philosophy. To Mr. Still, melody is the factor of primary importance. Next in priority comes harmony, form, rhythm, and dynamics. In music the exotic is desirable, but one should not lose sight of the conventional in seeking new effects. Dissonance does have a value and can be used with pleasing effects; it is a spice that should be used in careful proportions. Our contemporary music can be, and should be, an expression of a world that is not necessarily ugly. Music should be an enriching factor in our lives. Mr. Still strives to create music that people will understand, appreciate, and enjoy. The public is the final judge of what will live and what will not live.

Style of composition. In 1931, John Tasker Howard commented on Still's individuality: "He has established himself as a serious composer who utilizes the Negroid elements of jazz. Quasi-modern, he is seeking an individual idiom halfway between the ultra-modernists and the conservatives." [1] Mr. Still's compositional style is many-faceted. His well defined forms and use of "give-and-take" texture are derived from eighteenth century Neoclassicism. The richness of his harmonies and texture along with the high level of emotional content in his works tend to mark him as a Neo-romanticist. The harmonic vocabulary employed in some of his compositions is derived from the Modern idiom. Mr. Still possesses the rare ability to synthesize the best elements of the old and of the new into compositions that are fresh, meaningful, and expressive.

Historical style continuum. In the historical style continuum of American music, William Grant Still may be placed as a Neo-romantic composer who displays tendencies to move in the direction of the Modern idiom.

William Grant Still, the man. William Grant Still is a musician's musician and a composer's composer. He is a highly self-demanding individual who seeks to obtain perfection in his compositions. In this regard he feels that "nothing ever is; it is always becoming." [2] He is a tireless worker, a tender father, and a devoted hus-

---

[1] John Tasker Howard, *Our American Music* (3rd ed.; New York: Thomas Y. Crowell Co., 1947), p. 455.
[2] Personal interview, Slattery-Still, 1969.

53

band. He is a totally dedicated composer and yet he does not take himself too seriously. Mr. Still possesses a quick wit and a keen sense of humor; he will quite readily poke fun at himself in a good natured way. Socially, he is without dissonance. He feels that he can improve race relations by doing the best job possible in his chosen field—the creation of beautiful music for all men to enjoy. Mr. Still is blessed with a balanced and well-rounded personality, a trait which is not always found in men of genius calibre. The prime motivator in the life of William Grant Still is his love of God, his people, and humanity. The genuine humbleness of this gifted composer is expressed by the phrase which he attaches to every composition, large or small:

"With humble thanks to God, the source of inspiration."

P. H. S.

THE VOCAL WORKS

REVIEWING THE VOCAL WORKS WHICH PARALLELED
THE CREATION OF
WILLIAM GRANT STILL'S SYMPHONIES

Of his two loves—opera and symphony—William Grant Still found opera the more compelling. Just as when he was a youngster studying the violin, he no sooner learned to read notes than he wanted to write them, so on hearing his very first operatic recordings in his early teens, he resolved that this was the sort of music *he* wanted to compose. Boylike, he went ahead and tried, even though at that time he had had so little preliminary training.

He entered contests for composers, carefully making his own manuscript paper when there was no printed paper available to him. Some of the contests were for original operas. When his entry for one of these was returned, the judges sent a note saying his work had merit, though they couldn't completely understand it. On another occasion, the judges returned his "opera", asking what on earth he had sent them! No wonder, for this ambitious effort was a scant twenty pages long.

The rejections did not dampen his enthusiasm, however. As the years went on and his formal training progressed, he wrote more and more operas and then discarded them when he decided they were not good enough. In perspective, he was able to act as his own judge and jury. Today he has even forgotten the names of many of those works. To him, they exist simply as exercises in composition which paved the way for works he *did* consider good enough.

Meanwhile, as he worked on opera after opera, he was also trying to make the connections which would make it possible for him to get public hearings in this medium, but he was constantly frustrated. Operahouses were few and were largely devoted to repeating those European operas which had won favor in the past. Many leading American composers found it impossible to break this barrier, and in Still's case there was the added difficulty of color.

At long last, he was forced to accept the fact that he could not break into the musical world that way, so he turned to writing symphonic music, and in this field he *was* successful. Nonetheless, his early desire persisted. He still wrote for voices (even including vocal sections in three of his four ballets) and he still wrote opera and more opera, until he finally was able to get some of it to public attention.

Notably, in the Twenties, his vocal works were *Levee Land* which won great acclaim in 1926 when sung in concert at Aeolian Hall by the incomparable Florence Mills, with Eugene Goossens conducting the orchestra, a concert attended by such luminaries as Arturo Toscanini, George Gershwin, Carl Van Vechten and many others—also the large-scale African choral ballet *Sahdji*, dedicated to and first performed by Dr. Howard Hanson in Rochester. This, too, was received with enthusiasm by public and press.

The successes of these works helped to bolster his basic passion for the writing of operas, but here, he soon found that another of his problems was the same as that of many other contemporary composers: getting a suitable libretto. He did not want to adapt plays that had been successful as plays, as some other composers did in later years, and he did insist that whatever he attempted had to be good theatre. Accordingly, he approached several Negro poets, asking for libretti but, for one reason or another, they promised but did not deliver. Then he tried writing a libretto of his own, called *Chloe*, set in Mississippi in modern times. Its plot dealt only with the conflict in the lives of several individuals and had no sociological connotations whatever. However, this too, he discarded.

Finally, he was awarded a fellowship specifically to compose an opera. He came from New York to the West Coast to work with librettist Bruce Forsythe on a scenario supplied by Carlton Moss. From this effort emerged *Blue Steel*, in three acts, a story of a mysterious voodoo cult in an inaccessible swamp, at odds with a strong-muscled, arrogant man from the outer world. Granted, the plot smacked of the particular sort of sensational elements that were joyfully accepted on the stage of the Twenties and Thirties— but it also contained popular elements that later led the composer to feel that the story itself would not make a lasting contribution. For that reason, he discarded the opera once it was completed, and later made use of sections of its music in other works.

This was a wise decision, for the music itself was unique: lush, exotic and appealing in melodies, harmonies and rhythms. It was composed at a time when its creator was fresh from the confines of commercial work, with many plans made and many preliminary sketches in his notebook. He was, in short, bursting with ideas and eager to get them down on paper. Inspiration flowed, morning, noon and night, and for as long as the work continued, *Blue Steel* was a pet project. In fact, one night immediately after it was completed, several singers (friends) came to his home to sight-read the score. As their voices rose and fell in the to-them unfamiliar music, its inspired quality became evident to all, even the neighbors who sat on their front porches to listen and applaud. The composer knew at that moment that he had not been wrong all along. *This*, indeed, was his field, and in this field he meant to persist, despite opposition.

Other compositions, mostly instrumental, occupied Dr. Still in the mid-Thirties, at the same time that there came a new operatic ray of hope. Langston Hughes, who had been asked for a libretto long before, suddenly found he had an unused libretto on his hands, after all. He had written the text of *Troubled Island* for the composer Clarence Cameron White, who had then rejected it. At that point, Mr. Hughes' economical soul recalled the earlier William Grant Still request, so he brought his Haitian libretto to the West Coast. Still was only too happy to have a text based on the dramatic story of Emperor Jean Jacques Dessalines of Haiti. He and the poet immediately set to work to make it conform to Still's concept of the needs of the music: the proper places for arias, for the ballet, and so on. It developed into an opera of three acts, four scenes.

While Mr. Hughes was adapting his libretto to the new requirements, Dr. Still was creating his leit-motifs which would, of course, re-appear in various guises throughout the opera to clarify and emphasize the action. There was a harsh motif designating the ugly scars left on Dessalines' back by the whips of slave-drivers; a warm theme to express the slave-wife Azelia's love for Dessalines; glittering sensuous music to depict the illicit affair of Empress Claire with the Emperor's secretary; a motif for intrigue, another for the Voodoo rites, and still another for Martel, who was described as being a symbol of world peace.

Since *Troubled Island* is on a Haitian subject, one might conclude that the music would contain authentic Haitian material—and indeed, there really is a snatch of one authentic folk tune in the final act. But, generally speaking, such an obvious device failed to capture Still's fancy and in this opera, as in his earlier African ballet *Sahdji* and his Martinique ballet *La Guiablesse,* he tried to steep himself in the subject and then create his own musical material in that style and mood. As it turned out, it was a sound decision in more ways than one, because at that time, very little authentic African, Haitian or other West Indian material was available for study in this country. The field was then new and largely unexplored by North Americans.

Once completed, *Troubled Island* became, as the previous operas had become, a source of anxiety because again, despite the composer's undeniable symphonic successes, a performance seemed out of the question. Apparently, there were some who felt that this was an exalted field that should not be opened to him. But, while making efforts toward a production, Dr. Still was not content to be idle, and one important factor emerged from the creation of *Troubled Island* that was to have a significant effect on many of his future vocal works.

This happened when the librettist, having finished his libretto, went off to Spain. He was, for that reason, not available when the composer needed to make changes in the text—even, in one important instance, in the drama itself. Somehow, Dr. Still had to improvise. He wrote the necessary music and then asked me to set words to it. Neither one of us was sure that I could do it, for I considered myself then, as now, a journalist rather than a poet. However, I tried to fill the need, and the result made Act II Scene I one of the highlights of the opera. After that, we decided that I *could* be the librettist for succeeding operas since I had one attribute that many poets lack: a knowledge of music.

So, while awaiting a production of *Troubled Island,* William Grant Still wrote two operas, both on my libretti. One, *A Southern Interlude,* was short and set in our contemporary South. It, too, was later discarded and many of its elements were incorporated into another work. The other, *A Bayou Legend,* in three acts, has not been discarded. Instead, it was once revised and now also awaits production. Its plot was developed from an authentic legend of the Biloxi region, concerning a man who fell in love with a spirit. Although the characters in the opera are of French descent, the musical allusion to this is of a subtle, rather than a direct, nature. Nor is the music concerned with characteristics peculiar to the geographical area. Instead, its purpose is to describe and color the story. The plot has to do with simple people, caught up in a drama that ends tragically.

During the waiting years, Dr. Still also composed *And They Lynched Him On A Tree* for white chorus, Negro chorus, contralto soloist, narrator and orchestra, on a text by Katherine Garrison Chapin, a stirring work which pointed to ultimate brotherhood in America. A year later, also on a text by Katherine Garrison Chapin, he wrote *Plain-Chant For America* for baritone soloist and orchestra for the Centennial celebration of the New York Philharmonic Orchestra. This was a patriotic composition which, when converted into a choral work almost thirty years later, proved to be just as timely and moving as when it was first performed.

The mid-Forties were a time of many new works, many auspicious performances and one prize of national import (that given by the Cincinnati Symphony Orchestra for the best Overture to celebrate its Jubilee season). Yet there was also time for more vocal works. One of these was the choral composition *Those Who Wait*, a dialogue between soloists and chorus clarifying the racial problems of the day. Another, *Wailing Woman*, for orchestra, soprano and chorus, had a definite Semitic quality and emphasizes a bond between members of different minority groups. These two were based on my texts. Still another, also Semitic in flavor, was *The Voice Of The Lord*, or *Mizmor Ledovid*, for tenor, chorus and organ. This was a setting of the 29th Psalm, requested and performed by the Park Avenue Synagogue in New York City. Then there was *From A Lost Continent*, a unique suite for chorus in four sections, using syllables instead of words to impart an archaic flavor. It was inspired by accounts of Mu, the continent that once existed in the Pacific area. And, of course, there were the charming *Songs Of Separation*, a cycle of art songs for solo voice and piano, set to poems by five Negro poets: Arna Bontemps, Philippe-Thoby Marcelin of Haiti, Paul Laurence Dunbar, Countee Cullen and Langston Hughes—each one having to do with lovers who have separated. From the tropical languor of the Marcelin *Poeme*, set in its original French, to the pert sarcasm of Dunbar's *Parted* and the tenderness of Cullen's *If You Should Go*, this group of songs is unusual in that the composer carefully selected the poems from collections by the five poets and then placed them in sequence so that together they formed an effective unit.

This creative activity accompanied, but did not supplant constant efforts to get a production of *Troubled Island*. Finally, Leopold Stokowski became interested in it and offered to present it at the New York City Center of Music and Drama with which he had just become affiliated. He was as good as his word, and quickly started a campaign to arouse public interest and to give it the sort of presentation he felt it should have. Years were to pass, and Mr. Stokowski eventually resigned from the City Center. But the production itself, after many maneuvers and counter-maneuvers, did finally get underway. To its opening came a blue-ribbon audience, which at first sat quietly, waiting to be convinced—and then applauded warmly and continuously as the opera progressed. The composer was supremely happy; the stage director (Eugene Bryden) left New York for his home in California feeling that he had a hit on his hands, and the director (Laszlo Halasz) lost no time in asking for another opera.

The next morning the reviews appeared. It was obvious that the critics had banded together to overrule the audience's verdict. While they were in no sense unfavorable, they still (as Carl Van Vechten later wrote)* sat on the fence so that they could jump either way when they saw how things were going later. So *Troubled Island* despite its enthusiastic acceptance, was *not* permitted to open the door for more operatic performances.

Nonetheless, William Grant Still went home to write not one, but two, new operas. These were *Costaso* (in three acts, four scenes) and *Mota* (also in three acts, four scenes) both based on my libretti. Since Mr. Halasz also did not stay at the New York City Center, these too were unperformed.

In these new operas, the composer discovered, as he had discovered in working on *A Bayou Legend* and *A Southern Interlude*, that he worked better when he could have a firm hand in the precompositional stages of the work. For instance, once the locale of the opera and the germ of a plot is established, it is he who does all the research, both musical and otherwise, and this is *his* exclusively, in every sense. As he gathers his notes, the complexities of the plot begin to unfold, much of it determined by what the characters themselves would do under the same circumstances in life. Then he decides where the arias will come, and then I step

---

* "The critics hedge a little at first, rather than have to eat crow later. The principal thing to notice is the way the audience ate it up. It is never a bore. Of how many other operas can this be said?"

in to write the dialogue and to indicate the opening line of each aria. After that, he writes the music and my words are set *to* it, thus giving him freedom to write as he wishes, and not limiting his musical expression to a rigid series of lines.

Costaso's setting was one we both loved: Spanish-Colonial America, with its romance, its colorful costumes and its all-pervading religious aura. The *Ave Maria* at the end of the second act, is in my opinion, one of the most devout and uplifting pieces of music ever written. The plot of *Costaso* was evolved by us from a germ of an idea in a legend of Colonial New Mexico, and as the characters developed, they told their own story. The Spanish atmosphere throughout is so authentic that the music often gives the feeling of the folk, though there is no actual folk material employed.

Quite different was *Mota,* the succeeding opera. This too was an original story, set in ancestral Africa, with the conflict coming between individuals who represented stubborn tradition on the one hand, and progress on the other. In the end, the cunning exponents of tradition, led by the witch doctor, eliminate *Mota,* symbol of a better life, by means of what today would be termed a "rigged" trial. He is branded a young upstart and is asked, "If the world is left to such as you, what will happen to the rest of us?" In the end, the traditionalists lose too, for the sword of their vengeance cuts down more than the crusader. It also takes the life of the witch doctor's beloved daughter and, too late, he realizes that his own lust for power has turned back on him.

As for all of his operas, Dr. Still constructed miniature sets for *Mota,* so that he could best visualize the action while composing.

A three-act opera called *The Pillar,* on an American Indian theme, and several art songs (notably *Song For The Valiant, Song For The Lonely, Grief* on a poem by LeRoy V. Brant, and *Citadel* on a poem by Virginia Brasier) followed *Mota* and *Costaso,* in addition to *A Psalm For The Living,* for chorus. The latter was, again, a setting of my text (this one pre-written), having to do with the premise that our Father is not only in Heaven, but is living among us, guiding our footsteps and inspiring our earthly achievements. This reverent work has been performed repeatedly with great success. Its lovely opening cadence gives a hint of the melodic line to come. The *Rhapsody,* a suite in four movements for soprano and orchestra, followed closely. It details the growth of awareness in a girl who grows from carefree childhood into maturity and into a realization of her function, as a mother, in the world of brotherhood to come. It was a commissioned work. Somewhat different in concept was the succeeding four-part song cycle titled *From The Hearts Of Women*. In this, a child sang to her doll; a woman reached middle age; a girl gloried in being a coquette; and a woman lamented the death of her son. Both of these suites were set to my texts—or, to be completely accurate, my words were set to his music.

Then, in 1958, we completed another opera set in a locale which fascinated us: New Orleans. The principal character, Minette Fontaine, was a prima donna in the old New Orleans Opera Company, around mid-Nineteenth century. Her name became the name of our opera, though of course, we *created* Minette Fontaine. As far as we know, there was no actual singer of that name in the New Orleans of that period. We also invented the plot of the opera. Naturally, a colorful spot like New Orleans gave plenty of opportunity for interesting action and interesting settings: the French Market, the home of a social leader, a plantation near the city, and even a seance room in the home of a Voodoo priestess. Though there is a slave chorus, the drama itself is played out between the other characters, Minette (strong-willed and selfish) gaining what she wants, but in effect, losing in the end, in a poignant and bitter finale.

It was Dr. Fabien Sevitzky, then of the University of Miami, who (after he had given a first performance to Dr. Still's prize-winning composition *The Peaceful Land*) asked for a new short opera which he could introduce at his Fourth Annual Festival of American Music in Miami. It was a new experience for us: to have an opera requested and a performance secure before the work actually began! So we set to work and very soon *Highway I, U.S.A.*, in two acts, was completed. It was set in contemporary America, in the living quarters adjoining a filling station near the busy highway, and the theme was one of our favorites: a man and his wife who love *each other*, despite the interlopers who try to come between them. This, too, turned out to be a simple story about simple people, avoiding the Freudian pitfalls that beset so many of our modern dramas. The music is thoroughly American in flavor, direct and to the point. It was received with warm enthusiasm at the Miami premiere, and at subsequent performances in other parts of the country.

The variety of locales for the Still operas (the Bayou country, Haiti, Africa, Spanish Colonial America, New Orleans and American Indian land) automatically gave each one an individual musical flavor and style, though over all, the composer's own distinctive personal idiom prevailed. As the late Wladimir Bakaleinikoff once remarked, after hearing several Still compositions of different types, "Already I begin to hear *him*!" indicating that the composer had succeeded, as few other contemporaries had, in making his own individuality apparent in his music.

Only one major vocal work followed *Highway I, U.S.A.* This was the suite for bass-baritone soloist and orchestra called *Path Of Glory*, set to my text concerning the fall of the Aztec Empire after its leaders had turned away from God.

And what of the future? There is yet another opera in the process of conception. Dr. Still wants it to be a large, climactic work. What ultimate form it will take, and what its theme will be, even he is not now sure. But it *is* taking shape.

V. A.

THE VIOLIN WORKS

THE VIOLIN MUSIC OF WILLIAM GRANT STILL

While living and studying in New York City in the 1930's, we had often heard with great pleasure an evening broadcast of the WOR Mutual Broadcasting System entitled "Deep River." The very original, effective and beautiful orchestrations of Negro Spirituals and semi-popular music which made up the repertoire of these programs deeply impressed us. Later on, when we had moved to Los Angeles, we happened to discuss these remarkable broadcasts with our good friend, the noted American composer, Robert Russell Bennett, and he told us that it was well known "in the trade" that the orchestrator for "Deep River" was William Grant Still, the composer of the "Afro-American Symphony" and other major symphonic works. He also mentioned that Mr. Still was a fellow member of his in the American Society for Composers and Publishers (ASCAP) and lived in Los Angeles.

We looked up Mr. Still's telephone number and introduced ourselves soon after at his home. To our dismay we learned that he had almost always composed with a specific performance or performer in mind, and that since he had not chanced to meet solo violinists, he had not yet written in that form. However, his resourceful and gifted wife Verna suggested that some piano pieces that she had played might well suit the violin.

One in particular, the "Blues" from the "Lenox Avenue Suite" (a piano interlude of an orchestral work commissioned by CBS) interested us both, and Louis Kaufman made a version of this piece for violin and piano which pleased the composer and his wife, and which the Kaufmans later played in countless concerts in the United States, South America and Europe. It has always received an enthusiastic response from audiences and critics. Later Mr. Still orchestrated an accompaniment for this violin piece for performances on Columbia Broadcasting Systems "Invitation to Music" (conducted by Bernard Herrmann) and with the National Orchestral Association at Carnegie Hall (conducted by Leon Barzin). The critic, Robert Simon, of the *New Yorker* magazine wrote on February 26, 1944: "Mr. Kaufman and the orchestra added the "Blues" movement from William Grant Still's "Lenox Avenue Suite" to the great approval of the audience", and Henry Simon, the critic of PM noted on February 15, 1944: "As an encore Mr. Kaufman played the "Blues" movement from "Lenox Avenue Suite", which was the most typically American music of all in this evening of ' recognition' ". The "Blues" seemed to naturally attract radio performances. Louis Kaufman broadcast it with conductor Lou Bring on September 30, 1943 over NBC's coast-to-coast RCA program, "What's New". He also played it with Leigh Harline conducting the Ford Summer Hour program for the ABC Network. It has always been puzzling to us that Mr. Still's publisher would not publish this violin arrangement so that many other violinists who have asked us and the Stills for the music, could have it. But in spite of the joint Kaufman-Still efforts over many years—this enchanting work is still in manuscript.

Other works Mr. Still composed for violin have had quicker publication. The "Suite for Violin and Piano" (or orchestra) was published almost before performance by Delkas. This major work was written for and dedicated to us both, and is based on three works of art by noted Negro artists. The first movement, inspired by "African Dancer" (a large bronze female figure) by Richard Barthe which is in the collection of the Whitney Museum in New York City; the second movement was suggested by Sargent Johnson's handsome colored lithograph in the collection of the San Francisco Museum of Art; the third movement refers to "Gamin" (the bronze head of a small Negro boy) by Augusta Savage (the Rosenwald Fund). Incidentally all these art works are reproduced in Alain Locke's fascinating book, *The Negro in Art,* which was published in Washington, D.C. in 1940 by the Associates in Negro Folk Education.

Louis Kaufman premiered this Suite in Boston's Jordan Hall with pianist Vladimir Padwa on March 15, 1944, and on March 17th of the same year with the same pianist in New York's Town Hall. He played the premiere of the 'orchestral version' in New York on March 25, 1946 with the WOR Symphony, conducted by Emerson Buckley. We also played this Suite at the Annual Festival of Modern Music at the First Congregational Church in Los Angeles organized by Arthur Leslie Jacobs in May of 1944. Another orchestral performance was broadcast by the Standard Symphony program conducted by Henry Svedrofsky on September 23, 1945.

Other Still compositions which we have consistently performed since 1943 are the "Pastorela" (a tone-poem inspired by California) which was written for us, and the two shorter compositions, "Summerland" and "Here's One" (an effective arrangement of the Negro Spiritual of the same name). Louis premiered the 'orchestral version' with the CBS Symphony, conducted by Bernard Herrmann, over the Columbia Broadcasting System. He has also played the quartet version of "Danzas de Panama" which was written for the violinist, Elizabeth Waldo.

Some of these programmed Still compositions have had an unlooked for 'social significance' that had never occurred to us working musicians!

The *New York Times* and *Newsweek* magazine published photographs of Louis Kaufman and Mr. Still looking over music together. We were told by reliable reporters that this was the first time these publications had printed pictures of a "White" musician and a "Negro" musician together. Evidently each category had always been given "solo only" photographs. Helping to end that barrier seemed a good (although unexpected) result of our pleasure in working with the Stills.

One more dramatic change for 1945. For seven years before we had played in Jefferson City, Missouri, the nearby (Negro) Lincoln University had been requesting permission to buy tickets to the Civic Concerts. No reserved seats! For seven years the answer had been, "No". Then the Negro press announced our forthcoming recital and the fact that we regularly programmed the works of William Grant Still. The University again sent in a request to buy tickets for the Kaufman program adding they were especially interested in Mr. Still's music. To our delight the President of the Civic Music Association of Jefferson City, Mr. Richard Arens, replied, "They're going to Heaven with us. There's no reason why they shouldn't hear music with us!" So about 85 Negroes came to our concert, and they *all* came backstage to tell us this interesting tale, and to shake our hands and congratulate us. So did many of the White members of this now happily unsegregated audience, who said such normal behavior would make the city a better place to live in.

We had long hoped to record these compositions, so we were very pleased to meet Mr. Giveon Cornfield, the director of Orion Records in the summer of 1971. He thought it was a most worthwhile project to commemorate our friend's 76th year with a long-playing record devoted to all these "major and minor" compositions for violin and piano, with the addition of another work, an arrangement of a folk-song of North America—"Carmela". This is a brief "serenade", which nostalgically recalls the charm of Spanish California. It was most gratifying for us to have the personal supervision of the Composer for this recording, which was made in Los Angeles and produced by Giveon Cornfield, with the best of modern technical equipment for Orion Stereo Records.

To our great delight Melody Peterson wrote in the Los Angeles Times, "The homespun warmth and bounding energy of Still's compositional style are conveyed in an extremely forthright manner by the Kaufmans." This inspired our friends (and life-long Still admirers) Mrs. Joan Palevsky and Dr. Robert Haas to ask whether we could "put together" yet another record of Still's works. We did: the very remarkable work for harp, piano and strings, entitled *Ennanga*; the *Danzas de Panama* for string quartet; and a very fine group of songs, *Songs of Separation*, based on texts by notable Negro poets, and *Song for the Lonely*, which Still wrote to the poetic text of his gifed wife, Verna Arvey. We had the great good fortune to obtain the cooperation of the splendid French mezzo-soprano, Claudine Carlson for this recording, and the excellent pianist-accompanist Georgia Akst. So, in March, 1972 the wishes of Mrs. Palevsky and Dr. Haas became realities, and the above works were recorded for Orion.

Both public and critical response to these records has been gratifying.

William Grant Still's violin music has proved to be a significant contribution to the violin literature and has had an ever widening influence in furthering national international communication.

L. K. and A. K.

William Grant Still at Oberlin College, 1970.

William Grant Still receiving the honorary degree of
Doctor of Laws at the University of Arkansas, 1971.

The 1911 graduating class from M.W. Gibbs High School,
Little Rock, Arkansas. William Grant Still,
third from the left in the top row.

William Grant Still in the Wilberforce University string quartet,
seated on the right, with violin. About 1912.

William Grant Still playing the 'cello in New York, early twenties.

W.C. Handy's office in New York, William Grant Still seated on the left,
next to the stenographer. Early twenties.

William Grant Still conducting at the Black Swan Recording Company,
early twenties.

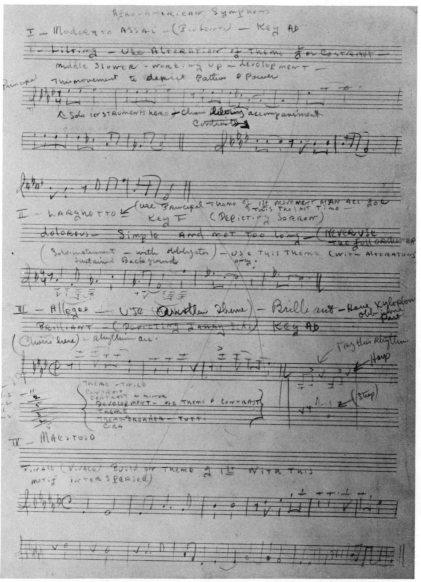

A page from William Grant Still's notebook, in preparation
for writing the AFRO-AMERICAN SYMPHONY. (Late 1920's, 1930.)

William Grant Still at the time of the Paris performance of AFRICA, 1933.

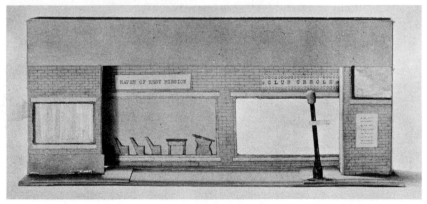

The cardboard set built by William Grant Still when he converted his composition, LENOX AVENUE, into a ballet. Mid-thirties.

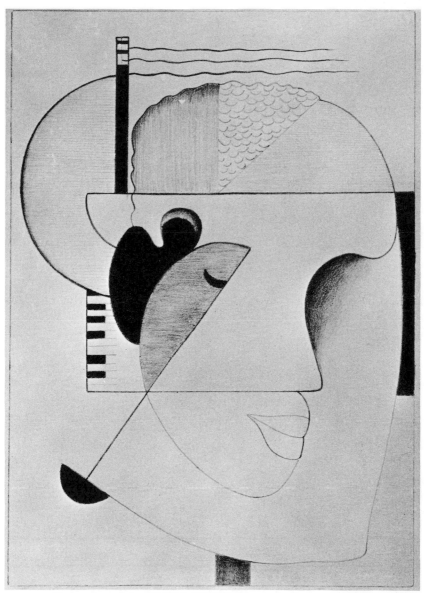

Abstraction of the LENOX AVENUE music, by Sargent Johnson,
San Francisco, 1938

Carl Van Vechten's photograph of William Grant Still at the time of the
New York production of TROUBLED ISLAND, 1949.

William Grant Still at work in his studio, early fifties.
Photo by LeRoy V. Brant.

Dr. Fabien Sevitzky with William Grant Still at the University of Miami
production of the opera, HIGHWAY 1, U.S.A. in 1963

William Grant Still conducting the Seattle Youth Symphony, 1968.

Dr. William Grant Still, Louis Kaufman - violin, Annette Kaufman - piano

Dr. and Mrs. William Grant Still at the Oberlin College celebration of his 75th birthday—seated. Three of the participants in the celebration were (left to right) Doris Mayes (mezzo-soprano); Natalie Hinderas (pianist); and Dr. Eileen Southern (author of the book, *The Music of Black Americans*)—standing. 1970

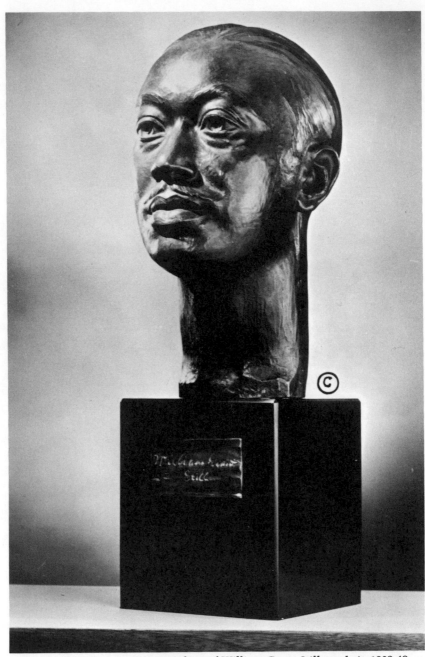

Joseph D. Portanova's portrait bust of William Grant Still, made in 1939-40.

THE STILLS ON STILL

MY ARKANSAS BOYHOOD

What with all the propaganda being disseminated nowadays, it may be hard for many people to believe that my boyhood was as it was—a typically American one, far removed from the ordinary concept of a little colored boy growing up in the South. I knew neither wealth nor poverty, for I lived in a comfortable middle-class home, with luxuries such as books, musical instruments and phonograph records in quantities found in few other homes of this sort.

All of this was the result of my having had the good fortune to have been born to intelligent, forward-looking parents, as well as to the fact that Little Rock, where I grew up, was considered by many of us to be an enlightened community in the South. This was true to such an extent that in later years, when the city's name was splashed over headlines the length and breadth of the world, those of us who had lived there were amazed and incredulous. We could not believe that of Little Rock, because it was contrary to so much that we had known and experienced!

It is true that there was segregation in Little Rock during my boyhood, but my family lived in a mixed neighborhood and our friends were both white and colored. So were my playmates. In many instances, their friendship lasted over into adulthood. Stanley and Clifford, for example, were two little white boys who played with me. Their father was a friend of my stepfather. Boy-like, we arranged an elaborate series of signals. We would have little flags or semaphores on our houses. These would be up when we were at home and down when we were away. This was so that we would not inconvenience our busy selves by calling on the others when the others were absent. When I returned to Little Rock in 1927, after my mother's death, Stanley (who then lived in North Little Rock) came back to see me.

So, while I was aware of the fact that I was a Negro, and once in a while was reminded of it unpleasantly, I was generally conscious of it in a positive way, with a feeling of pride. At the same time, my association with people of both racial groups gave me the ability to conduct myself as a person among people instead of as an inferior among superiors. The fact that this could be done at all in the South represents, to me at least, an open-mindedness on the part of so many of the other residents of Little Rock.

It would be completely unrealistic if I were to suggest that there were no incidents involving racial prejudice in Little Rock, because there *were*, and they did make an impression on me. I even witnessed one such occurrence, which today would be termed "police brutality" on Center Street. It horrified me, but did not change my feeling that the good people in Little Rock overbalanced the bad.

In shaping my attitudes, my mother had a most important role to play. She was constantly "molding my character," trying to keep me from "following the path of least resistance," impressing on me the fact that I *must* amount to something in the world (it never occurred to her or to me that any other course was possible, even though she and I had different ideas as to the means of accomplishing it), correcting my grammar and my accent, and never sparing the rod lest her child be spoiled.

If my father had lived (he died only a few months after I was born in Mississippi) he would have been expected to discipline me. But since he could not, my mother courageously set out to be both mother and father. She gave me chores to do: cutting the kindling and the wood, bringing it and the coal indoors; starting the fires every morning; sweeping the house. When in high school I wanted long trousers like the other boys, I had to go to work to pay for them. My mother could easily have given them to me, but it was part of her discipline to let me earn them.

That work was in an Arkansas heading factory, making barrel heads. It was exhausting, but I stuck to it until I got the trousers. One of my subsequent jobs was in an ice cream factory; another in a soda fountain where I could get lots of fizzy water to drink. Still another was in an electro-therapy office, where I nearly drove the doctors crazy, experimenting with their machinery in moments free from duty.

Although my mother was strict and proud, she had a sense of humor and she loved me dearly. I remember her discipline today with gratitude and affection.

My parents were far removed from the sort of colored people we now term the "stereotypes," and their circle of friends matched them in fine upbringing. They both were teachers in secondary schools in the South; both were musical; both were creative in

76

many ways. Charles B. Shepperson, the stepfather who came into my life when I was about eleven, was a postal clerk and a sensitive soul who loved the arts. It was he who bought Victor Red Seal records for our phonograph and took me to see the various stage shows that came to Little Rock. He initiated and fostered in me a love for the stage which has never died.

We had come to Little Rock, my mother and I, after my father's passing. We lived with my Aunt Laura (then Mrs. Oliver) at 912 West 14th Street. Later, my mother bought that house as well as other property in Little Rock.

This was a city comparable to other American cities of that era, with many fine homes, theatres and a thriving business section. Even so, it was not far removed from typical rural life: women in sunbonnets, farms, cane fields. About five miles out of the city was "Sweet Home," where I remember watching horses go 'round and 'round, crushing the cane to make sorghum.

This was around the turn of the century, and yet it was near enough to real frontier days to have sights that today would be unheard-of, such as the two dead bandits who were put on display in Little Rock as a method of deterring would-be criminals. One was a big white bandit who had tried to rob a little white railway clerk of his diamond. In the struggle, the mail clerk's .45 calibre gun went off when it was thrust up against the robber's chest. The big hole it made was left visible by the embalmers, so that we could see it plainly when the body was displayed in the funeral parlor's window. The other was a Negro bandit, whose body was also intended for display. One of my friends and I were enterprising enough to go to the funeral parlor during the embalming process and get a first-hand look. We never forgot it.

During my early years, my maternal grandmother also lived with us, and it was she who sang Spirituals and Christian hymns all day long as she worked. "Little David, Play on Yo' Harp" was her favorite. Outside of that, my early musical experience had to do with songs such as are sung in school, hymns heard in church, and pieces like the "Angels' Serenade"—later, when I began to study the violin at my mother's insistence. Negro music, as we know it today, was not yet an important part of my life.

As a matter of fact, it was so foreign to what I usually experienced that one summer, when I was still in elementary school, I accompanied my mother when she went to teach in Olmstead, a

77

rural community. These simple people had only a few weeks of school each year, and very few other advantages. Their schoolroom was topped by loose branches instead of a roof, branches which hid scorpions and any other form of insect life which felt that it wanted to take a closer look at learning.

Because she was a visiting teacher, my mother was expected to attend their social functions, one of which was a basket meeting on Sunday, in this case, an affair both religious and social. As a prelude to the variety of food prepared by the housewives, they all gathered in the church, sang Spirituals and shouted. I thought they were very funny and laughed heartily. My mother scolded me and sent me out of the church. The thought that I was "hearing authentic Negro music at its source" never entered my irreverent little mind. All I was interested in was the food. I considered the rest of it a hilarious show put on just for my benefit.

Back in Little Rock, my schooling—and that of my friends— was on a more dignified plane. I went first to Capitol Hill School which wasn't built on a hill at all, but was located in a section named Capitol Hill. It was a school of moderate size, with a main building of red brick back of which was an old-fashioned frame structure. In the schoolyard were many rocks and trees around which were built rough benches for the children's use during lunch hours. I always ate lunch with my mother, for she taught at Capitol Hill School too, but in the High School Department. In the 8th grade I was sent to Union School for a year, since we lived in that district.

Eventually, Capitol Hill School proved to be too small to be both a high school and a grammar school, so a new high school named after Judge M. W. Gibbs was built. My mother, of course, taught there.

Whenever I was enrolled in one of my mother's classes, such as literature, I suffered through every moment, and won the sympathy of *all* my fellow-students. Mama was determined not to let anyone accuse her of partiality; she was also determined that I *had* to excel. The slightest error found me standing in the corner, being given demerits, or feeling the sting of Mama's ruler as it cracked smartly over my fingers. This happened once when I was reading Chaucer aloud to the class and, coming to the word "dung," I laughed a hearty schoolboy laugh. That ruler was put into action immediately. When I pouted, she said, "Stick that lip in, young man!"

78

Each time I was involved in a childish prank, I could count on a whipping when I got home, and I was often involved because most of my schoolmates were just as impish as I. Once, but only once, I played hookey to watch the trains pass, and to see the horses being shod in the blacksmith's shop.

Today I can find it in my heart to feel sorry for poor Professor Gillam, whom all the boys loved to torment. We poured water in his chair before he sat down; hit him in the back with little pieces of crayon when he turned around to write on the blackboard. If we had stayed in that school a few years longer we would have regretted our practical jokes, for Professor Gillam eventually became Principal and was in an ideal position to retaliate. He forgave us, though, and became a good friend in later years.

Many times I had to escort my mother to club meetings when Mr. Shepperson wasn't at home, for though the people in our group danced and played cards as people do socially today, they also managed to support events of a cultural nature and to promote Negro artists. Clarence Cameron White, the colored composer, played the violin at one such program; Mme. Azelia Hackley (who helped many Negro artists get scholarships) gave a vocal recital; Richard B. Harrison, later to win fame as The Lord in "The Green Pastures", read a Shakespearian play; others came to lecture.

There were projects in which my mother took the lead and of course I was always expected to be on hand. At that time, my mother was disturbed over the fact that there was no public library in Little Rock open to colored people, despite the fact that several colored residents had extensive private libraries. So she organized performances of some Shakespearian plays, and with the proceeds bought books which formed the nucleus of the library in Capitol Hill School.

The violin was selected as my first instrument, possibly because I had been inspired to make toy violins when I was little. My first teacher was Mr. Price. Here again, it was my mother who insisted that I practice regularly. However, when I was elected Valedictorian of my class at Graduation time, my mother decreed that my speech should be memorized—which dismayed me to such an extent that she then had to beg me to stop practicing.

High school graduation found quite a few less members in my class than had entered school some years before. Many had left, one at a time, in order to take jobs and help support their families.

For me, college was the next step. And it was after I had enrolled in Wilberforce University that I decided that I *must* become a composer. My mother opposed this because, in her experience, the majority of Negro musicians of that day were disreputable and were not accepted into the best homes. She had wanted me to be a doctor. After many arguments she realized that my mind was made up: nothing but music would do.

After my college years, I was thrown out on my own, a fortunate occurrence as it later turned out, since I entered the field of American commercial music in order to make a living, and there learned many things which my later conservatory training could not and did not give me. It was in Columbus, Ohio that I first worked as a professional musician and it was there, while I was alone one day, that I decided to use whatever talent God had given me in His service. This was a promise which I made in my own way, and which —also in my own way—I have kept.

A few years and many experiences later, in New York, I began to feel that one way to serve God would be to serve my race. Then that in itself began to seem a narrow objective, so I decided that I wanted to serve *all* people. All three objectives, I thought, could best be achieved by doing whatever I had been sent on earth to do —in this case, music—to the very best of my ability, so that the accomplishment would in itself count for something.

The middle twenties had to arrive before I had committed myself to Negro music, however. This followed periods of conservatory study at Oberlin; learning in the school of experience (i.e., I was self-taught in orchestration); and private study on scholarships, with George W. Chadwick who acquainted me with serious American music, and with Edgar Varese, who introduced me to the ultramodern idiom. All the while, I had been making it a point to listen to Negro music everywhere I went. On Beale Street in Memphis, where I worked with W. C. Handy, as an onlooker in small Negro churches, and in popular bands.

Although my compositions in Mr. Varese's dissonant idiom brought me to the attention of metropolitan critics, I soon decided that this was not representative of my own musical individuality, and adopted a racial form of expression. Quite a few of my compositions with racial titles were the result of this decision. I made an effort to elevate the folk idiom into symphonic form, though rarely making use of actual folk themes. For the most part, I was

80

developing my own themes in the style of the folk.

Following this period, there came a time when I leaned toward a more universal idiom which, in my opinion, partook of all the others and became an expression of my own individuality as a composer. In other words, instead of limiting myself to one particular style, I wrote as I chose, using whatever idiom seemed appropriate to the subject at hand.

This surely would have won my mother's approval. She lived long enough to know that my initial serious compositions had been successful, and her pride knew no bounds. Although she had opposed my career in music, she finally understood that music meant to me all the things she had been teaching me: a creative, serious accomplishment worthy of study and high devotion as well as sacrifice. She knew at last that the ideals which she had passed on to me during my boyhood in Arkansas had borne worthy fruit.

W. G. S.

WITH HIS ROOTS IN THE SOIL

M ore than a quarter of a century ago, North Americans were busily engaged in a search for a serious composer whose works would most accurately reflect their country in music. As the search continued, many arguments occurred. What sort of music would be the most representative? Anglo-Saxon music? For everyone knew that all the countries in the Western Hemisphere had been settled by people of many different racial and nationalistic groups.

It seemed to some of the searchers that perhaps a blend of *all* types of music would best represent the melting pot that is the U.S.A. But how and where to find it?

Amid the arguments and the seeking, a composer who combined many of those elements within himself was working quietly, having his compositions played auspiciously at home and abroad, and slowly but surely winning recognition as a genuine American composer. This was William Grant Still, whose mother was of Negro, Spanish, Indian and Irish ancestry, and in whose father's veins flowed Negro, Indian and Scotch bloods. The son of this union naturally came into life with a heritage that was truly American in all its aspects.

More than that: he balanced his academic musical training with a practical experience in the field of American popular music. This happened because he was faced with the problem of making a living for himself and his family, and the commercial field appeared to be the most remunerative. But he also resolved to learn from it and to make use of its valuable assets in his own creative work. Small wonder that, when audiences abroad hear his music for the first time, they are apt to recognize it immediately as being a product of the North American continent. Some European critics have described it as the "most indigenous" music to come out of North America.

In writing about Americans of Negro derivation it has been the custom to mention their lowly beginnings or to dwell upon lurid aspects of their lives. It is not possible to do this in writing of William Grant Still; for his parents both were schoolteachers, both musicians, far removed from the folk. He was born on a plantation near Woodville, Mississippi, on May 11, 1895. When his father died, six months later, his mother took him to live in Little Rock, Arkansas, where she taught school and where he gained his elementary education.

In those years, Little Rock was known as an enlightened community, as compared with other places in the South. The boy thus had an opportunity to grow up among friendly people—people who were interested in cultural matters and who listened to him appreciatively when he began to play the violin.

Later, in Wilberforce University, he found many more appreciative friends when he started to lead the band, to train players for it, and to make musical arrangements for the band to play. It was then that he made his first timid efforts toward musical creation.

At the close of his stay at the college, he and his mother had a disagreement, as a result of which he left home and began to earn his own living in a strange city. Upsetting as this was, it undoubtedly had a profound effect on the music he was to compose later. Had he stayed at home, accepting his mother's bounty, he might have gone to a Conservatory of Music and there might have learned no more than the academic way of composing music. As it was, he chose to work among professional musicians, thus automatically absorbing a different approach to music than a Conservatory might offer.

Meanwhile, he realized that he must not neglect academic knowledge. So he went to the Oberlin Conservatory of Music, at times working to get enough money to pay for his tuition and at other times being the recipient of scholarships.

Later, he was given scholarships with two men of widely divergent musical tastes: George W. Chadwick of the New England Conservatory, a pioneer North American composer, and Edgar Varese, French ultramodernist. From each of them, he acquired valuable knowledge. Mr. Chadwick sharpened his own self-critical faculties, while Mr. Varese led him into new and untried paths of musical expression.

Meanwhile, the commercial work he engaged in (playing in orchestras, orchestrating for Broadway shows, conducting radio orchestras, and so on) supplied an education of an entirely different sort. Because of it, he was entirely self-taught in the field of orchestration. His desire to experiment and to create new orchestral tone colors quickly marked him as an innovator and a pioneer.

Many of the instrumental effects used today by other orchestrators actually stem from his early efforts.

He has considered it a blessing that he never learned to play the piano. Had he done so, he might have written first for piano and then orchestrated the piano scores. As it is, he now writes directly for orchestra, and his playing knowledge of orchestral instruments —the oboe, violin, and cello—has helped him to write playable and enjoyable parts for each instrument.

Before his study with Mr. Varese was over, Mr. Still had tried —and found wanting—many of those unusual ultra-modern experiments in sound that are still incorrectly labelled "music." He had become more dissonant than some of the acknowledged disciples of dissonance, to such an extent that those disciples hailed his early efforts joyfully. After a few of those compositions had been played in New York, however, the young composer began to have grave doubts about the value of the idiom, and particularly about its suitability for him.

Second Period

He then discarded dissonance for the sake of dissonance in favor of a Negroid musical idiom. This seemed to him to be more in keeping with his own individuality at the time. Some of the works he wrote after making that decision are still played and have become, in fact, among the best known of all his compositions. They are the *Afro-American Symphony, Africa, From the Black Belt* and the ballet *Sahdji*.

It was not long before he began to feel about the racial idiom exactly as he had felt before about the discordant idiom: that it was too confining, and that it should not be an end in itself. So, in the early thirties, he embarked upon a creative period which has not yet ended, and during which he has utilized any or all idioms which have seemed to suit the purpose of the particular composition he was writing at the moment—but always with a singleness of purpose and with good taste, never in haphazard fashion.

He still feels that this method is the answer to many of the problems arising among contemporary composers. If followed, it would bring variety to the concert hall and rekindle the waning flames of audience interest in new music.

For audiences happen to be one of the major interests of this composer. Not in the sense that he believes in "writing down" to people, nor in writing what is generally termed "popular" music. Rather, with the knowledge that an audience is, after all, the ultimate consumer of a composer's product, and that it must find in that product something that it needs and wants, or else it simply turns away.

Mr. Still believes that it is possible to compose serious music that is truly serious and yet will still fill an audience's needs. He deplores the ego which causes some composers to expect people to hear and applaud their works, whether worthy or not, as much as he deplores the insistence of some schools of musical thought that their way is the *only* way.

Another type of composer with whom Mr. Still is in disagreement is the one who listens too carefully and too often to other composers' works, with the idea of finding out what is being done currently, in order to follow the general trend. Mr. Still, on the contrary, tries not to listen to the works of others beyond getting acquainted with them, for fear of being influenced, consciously or unconsciously. It is not a disinterest on his part. Rather, it is a reluctance to assimilate what does not belong to him.

Similarly, he finds it hard to accept arguments over atonalism vs. nationalism in music. To him, there is something useful in both idioms. He finds dissonance effective when dissonance is needed (but he does *not* agree that dissonance is the sole end of all music) and he also finds a great deal of beauty in the various schools of nationalistic thought. Each nation in his opinion, has something distinctive and valuable to contribute to the world's cultural assets; each nation's composers, artists and writers should consider it a duty and a privilege to preserve their national heritage for posterity.

In the early thirties and afterward, when Mr. Still lived on the West Coast of the United States, away from New York and away from the compulsion to do as others in his field were doing, he wrote many compositions which demonstrated versatility in the variety and type of music composed. At the same time, he also succeeded in developing a decidedly personal idiom, one that is clearly recognizable as his in all his works. This is something that few composers in all history have achieved.

Closest to his heart are his operatic works, some of them as yet unproduced. Altogether, seven operas and four ballets have come from his pen, each one different from that which preceded it. Among the choral and orchestral works are many which express his own sharpened social consciousness, and his selection of subjects which speak of the brotherhood of man. Some of these are his *And They Lynched Him on a Tree* (for double mixed chorus, narrator, contralto soloist and orchestra); *In Memoriam: The Colored Soldiers Who Died for Democracy* (for orchestra); *Rhapsody* (for soprano and orchestra): *The Little Song That Wanted to be a Symphony* (for narrator and orchestra, a work for children) and so on.

Such compositions as *Poem for Orchestra* and *A Psalm for the Living* are the outgrowth of one of his earliest ambitions: to be able to serve God with his creative ability and to try in every way to make his music point to the Supreme Creator. It is for this reason that every one of his scores, from the smallest to the five symphonies, bears the inscription, "with humble thanks to God, the Source of inspiration."

His work for piano, such as the *Three Visions* and *Seven Traceries* are reminders of his early interest in the modern idiom, yet are distinctly personal in their harmonic treatment. For this composer is one who does not believe that harmonic resources have now been exhausted. With a little searching, a true creator can open up vastly new horizons without going to extremes in the matter of discords.

Another fertile field for investigation has been the folk music area. Not only has Mr. Still interested himself in setting North American Negro Spirituals but also in arranging some of the ingratiating melodies coming from other countries in the Western Hemisphere, such as his string quartet, "Danzas de Panama," his "Miniatures," "Vignettes" and Folk Suites nos. 1, 2, and 3, for various small chamber ensembles.

During his lifetime, this composer has received many honors: honorary degrees from four universities in the United States, commissions from the League of Composers, Paul Whiteman, the Cleveland Orchestra and the Columbia Broadcasting System. In 1939 he was selected to write the Theme Music for the New York World's Fair; in 1944 he won the Cincinnati Symphony's prize for the best overture to celebrate its Jubilee season; and in 1961 he won the prize offered by the National Federation of Music Clubs and the Aeolian Music Foundation for a composition dedicated to the United Nations. This was *The Peaceful Land,* introduced by Fabien Sevitzky and the University of Miami Symphony Orchestra. On May 13, 1963, his new one-act opera, "Highway No. 1, U.S.A.," was given its premiere at the close of the University of Miami's fourth annual Festival of American Music. Mr. Still is today a respected member of ASCAP, and a life member of Local 47, A. F. of M.

The Simple Life

He prefers to live and work simply and quietly at his home in Southern California, where he fills each day with a varied assortment of chores. In the morning, music. In the afternoon, constructing useful objects for the home, tending the plants. His interest in young people has been stimulated by his own children, so that of recent years he has composed several works especially for youngsters. Occasionally, he leaves home to conduct his own works, or to speak. That he has a genuine message for listeners is apparent not only in his music, but in his clear-thinking approach to matters of musical moment.

Contemporary audiences have so often been told that they *must* accept what is known as "ultra-modern" music and art, that they breathe a sigh of relief when an authoritative voice tells them they do not indeed have to accept what they do not like. Nor do they have to force themselves to listen to people or music whose sole virtue is that of having been publicized out of all proportion to its true worth. Merit should be the only basis for advancement, and the day will come, Mr. Still firmly believes, when it will be.

His is a warm, sincere and friendly personality, even as is his music. So it is fitting that he has dedicated himself and his work to the task of bringing men together in brotherhood. Successful thus far, he hopes only that his work will have made a resounding contribution to that goal when the last note has been played and the last song sung.

V. A.

MEMO FOR MUSICOLOGISTS

It was with considerable surprise that I read in a recent book (*Music in the 20th Century*, by William W. Austin, published by W. W. Norton and Company, 1966) by a Cornell University professor, the statement that "Gershwin's Rhapsody helped inspire William Grant Still to make use of Jazz and Negro folksong in his symphonies and operas." Surprise, because it seemed so unrealistic to assume that a Negro composer could have been motivated by a white composer who had made no secret of his own devotion to Negro musicians and their music.

For Gershwin's indebtedness has been well documented over the years, and it does no disservice to his memory to acknowledge it, since he himself did just that during his lifetime. One of these acknowledgements came when on August 30, 1926 he autographed a copy of his *Rhapsody in Blue to* W. C. Handy. "For Mr. Handy," he wrote respectfully (for at that time the beloved Father of the Blues was almost twice his age) "whose early 'blue' songs are the forefathers of this work. With admiration and best wishes."

Those people who lived—as did Gershwin—through the exciting Twenties in New York can attest to the presence of both Gershwins (George *and* Ira) at nearly every place where Negroes were performing, or even enjoying themselves at parties. As the veteran songwriter Jack Yellen put it in an article in the Autumn, 1966 issue of the *ASCAP News*: "Among the young white composers who frequented the hot spots of Harlem were the already-famous George Gershwin and a novice named Harold Arlen, and their visits undoubtedly influenced their subsequent compositions. It was soon thereafter that Gershwin wrote his classic *Rhapsody in Blue.*"

Kay Swift (herself the composer of the New York musical hit, *Fine and Dandy*, and often a sort of musical secretary to Gershwin) in an interview given for the April, 1948 issue of the West Coast magazine, *Opera and Concert*, told of going with George Gershwin at 3, 4 and 5 A.M., after their respective shows were over, to little places in Harlem where there were recordings by Negro artists that couldn't be gotten downtown. There Gershwin would listen intently, making mental notes and absorbing the style. She also told of the Macedonia Church in Charleston, where Gershwin used to go to hear the Gullah Negroes who formed the congregation sing (or shout) and to join in the singing and shouting. This is a fact also documented by Dubose Heyward in the chapter he contributed to Merle Armitage's book on Gershwin.

Also clarified by Miss Swift was the relationship between Gershwin and Will Vodery, the colored orchestrator who was so well established in New York when Gershwin was just starting. Their friendship initiated the rumor that Gershwin had a colored ghost writer—which was not true. What *was* true was that Vodery befriended Gershwin in the early days and—recognizing talent—got him a job with a big publishing house. Gershwin never forgot the kindness and later asked Vodery to orchestrate for him.

In addition to haunting spots where Negroes of the primitive type could be heard, Gershwin also made it a point to be present at any concert or show in which a Negro was doing something new in music. If getting there was difficult, according to Miss Swift, he would make the effort somehow and arrive in time to hear it. Thus it was inevitable that Gershwin should attend some of the early concerts in New York in which William Grant Still's music was featured. One such was at Aeolian Hall on January 24, 1926, given by the international Composers' Guild with the unforgettable Florence Mills as soloist and Eugene Goossens conducting.

This was an early effort to place the American Negro folk idiom in the context of concert music, the result of a dream of Still's dating back to 1916 when he, as a young man, went to Memphis to work with W. C. Handy. Before that, he had led a sheltered life with a family composed of teachers, civil service workers, and so on. Now the full impact of Negro folk music came to him as a welcome addition to his own formal musical training. On Gayoso Street, in Memphis, he heard for the first time unadorned Blues singing. However, he heard the Blues, not as something immoral and sexy, but as the yearnings of a lowly people, seeking a better life. Then and there he resolved that someday he would elevate the Blues so they could hold a dignified position in symphonic literature, and from then on he was making countless musical experiments toward that end—sometimes in the commercial arrangements he made for other people, sometimes in original compositions which he would write, revise and then discard as being not yet good enough. Most of these early efforts were lost before they were performed publicly, and more than a dozen years were to pass—years occupied with study, first-hand experience with orchestras, more observation of the Negro folk idiom, etc., before his dream finally crystallized in the *Afro-American Symphony*.

One Negro musical show which took New York by storm in the early Twenties was *Shuffle Along*. George and Ira Gershwin and most of the other Broadway celebrities attended it, some more than once. The Eubie Blake and Sissle orchestra was the one used in *Shuffle Along;* and, in it, William Grant Still played oboe. As the show went on and on, the players in the orchestra began to get tired of playing the same thing over and over again, so very often they would improvise. Most of them had a special little figure that they added, as they felt so inclined. Still's figure was melodic. Later, when he was composing the *Afro-American Symphony*, he used the same little figure, wedded to a distinctive rhythm which he had originated in the orchestration for a soft-shoe dance in the show, *Rain or Shine*. It became a brief accompanying figure in the Scherzo movement of the *Afro-American Symphony*, not at all related to the original theme in the Blues idiom on which Still had constructed the entire symphony.

Apparently, at the same time Still was composing the *Afro-American Symphony*, Gershwin was writing *Girl Crazy*, in which *I Got Rhythm* appeared, for that show and the *Afro-American Symphony* were brought to public attention about the same time (1930). Naturally, the people who had heard more about Gershwin than about Still assumed that the latter had copied the former in that tiny phrase.

Gershwin felt that he was not "borrowing" any musical material exactly. He was listening and absorbing, then transferring the Negro idiom to his own musical speech. Yet we might assume that sometimes there actually was unconscious borrowing, not only in the *I Got Rhythm* episode, but in others. How else can the similarity of the opening notes of his *Summertime* (in *Porgy and Bess*) to the opening notes of the *St. Louis Blues* be explained?

As composers, the difference between Gershwin and Still is obvious. Gershwin approached Negro music as an outsider, and his own concepts helped to make it a Gershwin-Negro fusion, lusty and stereotyped racially, more popular in flavor. Still's approach to Negro music was from within, refining and developing it with the craftsmanship and inspiration of a trained composer.

90

Gershwin and Stephen Foster and certain American songwriters were not alone among white musicians in their appreciation of the possibilities of Negro music. Years before, Antonin Dvorak had come to America and had written chamber works and the *Symphony No. 9* ("From the New World") which were so infused with the feeling of Negro music that ever since some people have been trying desperately to prove it was not so, while others have been trying just as hard to find precise Negro melodies which could have been the basis of his work. In the main, the latter has been an unsuccessful quest, for Dvorak (like Gershwin) discounted any conscious "borrowing." "All I tried to do," he claimed later, "was to write music in the spirit of national American melodies."

However, the presence and influence of Harry T. Burleigh, the colored composer, in Dvorak's life *cannot* be discounted. Mr. Burleigh for four years was a student at the National Conservatory in New York during Dvorak's tenure as its director. He repeatedly visited Dvorak at his home on East 17th Street in order to sing Plantation songs and Hoe-downs to him. There was no question in Burleigh's mind, the mind of Walter Damrosch and that of Camille W. Zeckwer of Philadelphia (another student in the Conservatory) as to what Dvorak had in mind. He repeatedly announced his intention to use Negro melodies in the "New World" symphony to all his students. He also, according to Mr. Burleigh, saturated himself with the spirit of the old tunes and then invented his own themes. Sometimes, when Burleigh was singing the Spirituals, Dvorak would stop him and ask if that was really the way the slaves sang.

One actual Spiritual, *Swing Low, Sweet Chariot,* did find its abbreviated way into the symphony in the second theme of the first movement, a sprightly theme in G Major, first given out by the flute. Mr. Burleigh remarked later that Dr. Dvorak had been especially fond of hearing him sing that Spiritual.

Wrote Dr. Dvorak himself in an article for *Harper's New Monthly* for February, 1895: "A while ago I suggested that inspiration for truly national music might be derived from the Negro melodies or Indian chants. I was led to take this view partly by the fact that the so-called plantation songs are indeed the most striking and appealing melodies that have yet been found on this side of the water, but largely by the observation that this seems

91

to be recognized, though often unconsciously, by most Americans."

Nor was the inclination toward Negro music confined to this famous example of the Czech composer and his Symphony. William Grant Still himself was startled when one of his later symphonies received its first performance on the East Coast, to read that it reminded one critic of Delius. At the time, Still was completely unfamiliar with Delius' music. But much later, in the book, *Delius as I Knew Him*, by Eric Fenby, published in London in 1937 by G. Ball and Sons, Ltd., he found this paragraph: *"Ol' Man River* and other such records gave him great pleasure, for the singing was reminiscent of the way his Negroes used to sing out in Florida, when as a young orange planter he had often sat up far into the night, smoking cigar after cigar, and listening to their subtle improvisations in harmony. 'They showed a truly wonderful sense of musicianship and harmonic resource in the imaginative way in which they treated a melody,' he added. 'And, hearing their singing in such romantic surroundings, it was then and there that I felt the urge to express myself in music.' "

Add to this the names of composers like Debussy, Ravel, Tansman, Milhaud, and even Brahms. The book, *The Unknown Brahms*, by Robert Haven Schauffler, published by Crown Publishers in New York in 1940, carries a statement by Arthur Abell, an American violinist who was one of the few who could inspire the master to talk intimately of his own work. "A year before Brahms died," said Mr. Abell, "he asked me whether I played the banjo. 'No,' I replied. 'Why?' 'Because at Klengel's I met an American girl who played for me, on that curious instrument, a sort of music which she called Ragtime. Do you know this?'—and he hummed the well-known tune which goes to the words:

> "If you refuse me,
> Honey, you lose me."

'Well,' the master continued with a faraway look in his eyes, 'I thought I would use, not the stupid tune, but the interesting rhythms of this Ragtime. But I do not know whether I shall ever get around to it. My ideas no longer flow as easily as they used to!' "

Brahms' inclination toward Negro music was no more than that—just an inclination which never found fulfillment. But the experiences of other white composers in the Negro idiom would lead one to accept the statement made by Carl Van Vechten in *Parties*: "Both critics and public are so unaware of the Negro origin of much American dancing that they continue to revive the hoary old lament that the Negro cannot create anything for himself, but must continue to imitate the white man's creations. A scrutiny of the facts must bring us to the inevitable conclusion that neither in music nor in dance is the Negro the imitator."

V. A.

STILL OPERA POINTS THE WAY

A new feather adorns the cap of the New York City Center Opera Company as a result of last season's successful presentation of William Grant Still's opera "Troubled Island," based on a libretto by Langston Hughes. Warren Storey Smith, distinguished New England music critic, wrote in the Boston *Post* for April 17, 1949, that this opera is not only "better than the general run of American operas," but also "a better show than that current sensation of the Lyric Theater, Benjamin Britten's 'Peter Grimes.'"

Certainly "Troubled Island's" success with its audiences and the ovations it received at its two initial performances have made Laszlo Halasz and other City Center officials decide on a policy of furthering the cause of native American opera in forthcoming seasons. It is not the first time that a stage work by William Grant Still has paved the way for other American music. For instance, when the American Music Festivals were started in Rochester, they consisted solely of music. Then, in 1931, Dr. Hanson decided to test audience reaction to a new venture and, together with choreographer Thelma Biracree, he presented Mr. Still's impressive African choral ballet, "Sahdji." So successful was it that ever since, one entire Festival night in Rochester has been devoted to American ballets—others by Mr. Still ("La Guiablesse" and "Miss Sally's Party") being presented incidentally.

The story of the opera "Troubled Island" begins back in its composer's boyhood. Early in his life, William Grant Still, fascinated by the music on the Red Seal records owned by his family, decided to write operas. He grew to love the theater so much that he used to sneak backstage in the theater in Little Rock, Arkansas, where he then lived. He even loved the smell of a theater: musty, old and, to him, tremendously appealing! When he was in college, he made trips to Dayton, Ohio, to hear operas performed, and one of his greatest thrills came when he heard "I Pagliacci" done in Cincinnati. All of these things were directed toward gaining knowledge that would help him later in composing operas, as were his readings of plays and study of dramatic technique, in addition to his actual contacts with the theater as a member of pit orchestras and as arranger for Broadway shows in his early professional

94

years. Then, in the belief that in order to learn to walk one must first attempt walking, he began to write operas and, one by one, to tear them up. "Troubled Island" was the second opera he considered good enough to keep, and to try to get produced.

When both he and Langston Hughes were living in New York, Mr. Still asked the poet to supply him with a libretto for an opera. This did not come at once, but several years later, when the composer had moved to California, Mr. Hughes came to him and outlined the plot of an opera to be based on the life of Jean Jacques Dessalines, the Haitian liberator. (He had previously written a play called "Drums of Haiti" on this subject, and now proposed to convert it into an opera libretto.) Mr. Still was strongly gripped by the bare recital, and agreed to write the music.

In the company of friends, the two artists went to a cabin in the California hills, and there the composer indicated the position of arias, choruses and so on. Mr. Hughes then returned to New York. After some months had passed (during which Mr. Still was eager to get to the composition of the music, but had no libretto to work from) he again came to California, settled down in a hotel room, left orders that he was not to be disturbed until 11 A.M. every morning and there, in a prosaic setting quite different from the pastoral countryside in which the libretto had been first outlined, turned out his libretto quickly. After that he left California to go to Madrid, which was then in the throes of war.

From that point on, work on the opera belonged entirely to Mr. Still. The music was begun in 1937, when a portion of Act I was completed. An extension of an earlier Guggenheim Fellowship made it possible for the composer to resume work in 1938, during which year the actual creation of the music was completed. A portion of 1939 was devoted to completing the orchestration. The work was interrupted only by a commission to write the theme music for the Perisphere in the New York World's Fair, and it was on one of the composer's visits to New York for the purpose of finishing the Theme Music that Robert Weede first saw, and sang at sight, excerpts from the principal baritone arias in "Troubled Island." Kay Swift, of the New York World's Fair staff, had introduced the two men. The composer was thrilled by Mr. Weede's voice and decided then that he would like to have him create the leading role in the first performance of the opera. This he actually did, eleven years later, giving a powerful performance, and adding to

95

his already-great stature as an artist.

During the creation of the music, Mr. Still spent many hours in research, only to discover that at that time there was almost no authentic Haitian musical material to be found in the United States. Accordingly, with the exception of two native themes (a Meringue, used in the last act; and a Voodoo theme, greatly altered, in Act I) which were supplied by John Houston Craige, author and former U.S. Marine officer stationed in Haiti during the occupation, all the themes and their various treatments were original with Mr. Still. He devised his own musical idiom to fit the subject and the locale.

Creatively, there were many things to be borne in mind while the music was coming into being. Some of them will bear noting here. Believing that opera is primarily entertainment, Mr. Still tried to write music that would arouse an emotional rather than a cerebral response in his hearers. He thought always of those who would listen to the finished product. "The latter statement," he once declared humorously, "does not include other composers!"

Harmonically, Mr. Still employed both consonance and polytonality with a view to maintaining interest and to achieve a sort of unity through the use of diversified styles. To each act, moreover, he gave a distinct musical flavor—but managed to retain an over-all effect of one-ness.

Especially did he try to make the recitatives more interesting by constructing the vocal lines on the motives having a direct bearing on the action of the moment or upon the thoughts underlying the words. He tried to let the text be clearly understood by approximating musically the speed and rhythm of the natural speaking voice and to have the music conform to the inflection of each word as it would be spoken. He also departed from tradition by restricting the recitative—that is, limiting its freedom by making it more metrical.

He chose his themes thoughtfully. For example, there is a re-iteration of notes in both the Azelia and intrigue themes, but they are quite different. One (Azelia) is working for Dessalines and the other (intrigue) works against him. Today, a reference to the composer's original notes show that all his themes underwent extensive alterations before emerging in their final forms.

Mr. Still divided his working hours into creative effort (sometimes he wrote only 1½ measures a day, sometimes as many as 25 measures, and generally around 12) and into mechanical work—the latter consisting of making the final piano-vocal score on the music typewriter, and on master sheets so that it could be reproduced by a black and white blueprint method, and also of orchestrating, extracting chorus and orchestra parts, and so on. The opera was scored first by its composer for very large orchestra, later re-scored for a smaller group. In all this, Mr. Still was a lone wolf—not even calling in an outside copyist. He also made his own miniature sets for each act, to gauge the action. These have since been destroyed.

The opera is set in the year 1791. The Haitian slaves led by Jean Jacques Dessalines, revolt against their masters. Azelia, Dessalines' slave wife, stands by his side in all his dangerous enterprises, but as soon as he becomes Emperor, he casts her off and lives in splendor with his lovely mulatto Empress, Claire. His downfall begins when he, through ignorance and shortsightedness (he wants freedom for the blacks only, while his aged African counsellor, Martel, dreams of a world where *all* men will be free) he is unable to prevent the secret plot against him, by his Empress and those members of his court who wish to supplant him. The sumptuous banquet of state, at which the slightly sardonic Minuet is danced by mulatto girls trained in Paris, is interrupted by a voodoo dance and voodoo drums from outside: an insistent throbbing that bodes ill for Dessalines. Dessalines rides to quell the uprising against him. In a distant marketplace by the sea he meets his traitorous generals and is on the point of winning a duel with one of them when another shoots him in the back. His body is left in the square to be robbed by ragamuffins and to be wept over by Azelia who, now crazed by her harrowing experiences, alone remains faithful to her husband, that broken Dessalines who once had all Haiti at his feet.

Because his librettist remained in Madrid, Mr. Still called upon his wife, a journalist, to supply alterations and additions to the libretto when they were needed. To her also fell the job of playing over for him, on the piano, the music that had been written every day, so that he could hear it objectively and study it with a view to improvements.

Once written, the question of a production came up, and for many years thereafter, it remained an unsolved question. It was twice submitted to the Metropolitan, whose rejection was "In advising you that, to our regret, we do not see our way clear to accept this work, we should like to point out that this conclusion should in no way be taken as implying any criticism as to the artistic merit of the work." After other rejections, Leopold Stokowski became interested in the work and wished to produce it. At City Center he joined with Mayor La Guardia, Newbold Morris, Mrs. Franklin D. Roosevelt and others to establish a fund for its production. Eventually the fund was discontinued, the money returned to donors all over the country. But Mr. Stokowski's enthusiasm had communicated itself to Laszlo Halasz, who finally decided to produce it and who, with Eugene Bryden to stage the work and with a large and cooperative staff, at last brought it to the public.

It must be added that some of the metropolitan critics hedged as to the opera's real worth, despite the ovation it received from the audience. Years before, Puccini had had the same experience with many of his operas, notably "La Boheme" of which critic Carlo Bersezio, writing in the *Stampa*, said "even as it leaves little impression on the minds of our audience, it will leave no great trace on the history of our lyric theatre." The New York critics did, however, term "Troubled Island" interesting, imaginative, atmospheric, and colorful. They also spoke of its "music of sensuous richness" and its "structure of considerable breadth" and "melodic curve" which commended it to the audience. Carl Van Vechten wrote to the composer afterward that "It is never a bore. Of how many other operas can this be said?"

Our State Department recorded "Troubled Island" for distribution abroad and presented recordings of its dress rehearsal on a Voice of America broadcast.

All in all, an important step forward for William Grant Still, and for Laszlo Halasz and the New York City Center!

V. A.

MODERN COMPOSERS HAVE LOST
THEIR AUDIENCE: WHY?

Early in 1956, a visiting European composer declared in a Los Angeles interview that "The composer today is in a situation that has never before occurred in musical history. We have completely lost our audience."

Soon after that, the music critic on another Los Angeles paper wrote that "Today's American composers, at best, encounter patronage rather than championship. And their greatest enemy is blank indifference."

Surprising? Not to those of us who had long noted the trend and had been sounding warnings—warnings that had all too often gone unheeded. Year after year, we spoke of the fact that the public was making known its likes and dislikes by the simple expedient of attending, or not attending, concerts.

Laymen were expressing their disapproval by writing letters to editors; artists such as Geraldine Farrar were saying that they did not care for "that sort of calculated noise"; even music teachers (who had tried hard to understand and appreciate the so-called "new" trend) were frequently having to admit that they had failed to grasp it, or to make their pupils accept it.

One of them confessed, in print, that she much preferred jazz!

And yet, year after year, the propagandists of meaningless music continued to insist that their products—and only their products—HAD to be accepted whether anyone cared for them or not!

It is just such a ruthless spirit that must animate dictators, and it may be that same spirit that antagonises audiences, when they are asked to listen to music that they have rejected time and time again.

It does no good to present this music as the "new" music, the "music of the future." It has been so labelled for more than forty years, and is less successful now than it was at its outset.

When it first came to public notice, this type of music was electrifying. What not everyone realised after that was that it succeeded because its dissonance had a reason for existing. For dissonance does have a value, and can be used with pleasing effects. Later, when some composers began to write dissonance just for the sake

99

of dissonance, there arose a sameness in the greater part of the music that was composed. Rare was the composer who succeeded in developing an idiom recognizable as his own; most of the contemporary music fell into a seldom-varied pattern.

It became the fashion to write thus and so, and those who did not follow the fashion slavishly were disparaged. Their music was sneeringly termed "popular" and "reactionary." Many people claimed to be seeking a musical Messiah, who would shed light on the contemporary musical situation, but whenever anyone dared to speak out, he was met head-on by the pronouncement of the dominant group.

Mathematical formulae were often used by certain of the leading contemporary composers as a basis for musical creation. (How the inspired composers of the past would have scorned such mechanical devices!) The intellect usually took precedence over the emotions, and while intellect is necessary to musical creation, it should be no more than subordinate to inspiration. Even when some of the composers spoke or wrote of the importance of inspiration, it was not always apparent in their works.

The demand for inspired music has had its effect, however. Some composers, long steeped in the intellectual tradition, have felt the need to respond in some measure and have devised long statements to describe and justify their methods. Nonetheless, words cannot disguise the basic qualities of music. Simply saying something is devout and spiritual does not make it so. Simply declaring that a succession of notes is a melody does not make it a melody, nor a few odd beats a recognisable rhythm.

These things the public senses intuitively because the public is, after all, the final judge of what will live and what will not live. It resents being forced, it refuses to be intimidated. Just as the spark of freedom burns in the hearts of people all over the world, whether they be free men or oppressed, so does the inner love of beauty, and so does the public appreciation of all that is worthy in the arts.

Because the public *is* beginning to express its wishes now, it will soon be able to hear contemporary music that it can and will enjoy, music that is contemporary because it is composed *now* and because it is the expression of a modern world that isn't necessarily ugly.

Such music is being written by composers who are waiting a

chance to make their products known to the world, free of sneers and false propaganda.

We venture to predict that among them there is indeed a composer whom God (not man) has appointed, probably unpatronised and unpublished by commercial interests.

As our musical horizons broaden, we may find this composer. But the horizons *must* broaden. We cannot limit ourselves to what a small group insists has to be our "new" music and expect a miracle to come from it. It hasn't happened yet, and the chances are it never will!

As Ivor Brown wrote from London (in an article titled "And Why Not Write of Daffodils?" in the *New York Times* Book Review for February 18, 1951):

"The skies are still blue and the grass is still green where war does not befoul them, and there are vast tracts of decency and compassion in the great continent of human nature. Let the writer continue to say so, unfevered and unabashed . . . And we should not have to find our relief in the serenity and sagacity of the classics alone. The contemporary writer can offer confirmation of our values of truth, beauty and wit by being true to his own way of narrative, play-writing, reflection, or poetry. He will do so far more effectively by believing so than by tearing up his technique, by making anarchy in art his reaction to anarchy in world affairs, and by meeting chaotic facts with chaotic composition."

If we substitute the words "contemporary artist" or "contemporary composer" for Mr. Brown's "contemporary writer" we will have just as true a statement. And if we accept his suggestion, we will soon find that modern music will have regained its audience. But it undoubtedly won't be the same music we have been taught to call "modern" for, lo! these many years.

V. A. and W. G. S.

101

NOTE: "One other who must be mentioned in speaking of the development of arranging for radio is Willard Robison, who conducted a show called 'Willard Robison and His Deep River Orchestra' on most of the networks some years ago. Mr. Robison's orchestra was a small one, but the effects he attained with it were so unusual and distinctive as to gather great attention not only from the public, but from other radio conductors and arrangers. I am told that the distinctive quality of his orchestra was first set by a then unknown symphonic composer, who is currently engaged in scoring films on the West Coast." From the chapter on "Arranging Music for Radio" by Tom Bennett in *Music in Radio Broadcasting,* edited by Gilbert Chase, McGraw-Hill Book Company, Inc., 1946, p. 78.

As most people in New York knew, it was William Grant Still who was both arranger and conductor of the Deep River Hour.

The speech which follows is an early one William Grant Still delivered at the Eastman School during the time of his orchestral innovations for the Deep River Hour—which, by the way, have been widely imitated through the years, so that today they no longer sound unique.

R. B. H.

ON ORCHESTRATION

D r. Hanson's invitation to tell you of my theories of orchestral scoring led me to discover that I had given but little, if any, thought to formulating such theories. Of course, they existed. But I had been so busy trying to learn more of the art of orchestration that I was not conscious of them. Although what I am about to say may seem paradoxical, it is nevertheless true. The more I learn of orchestration the more I know how *little* I know of it. Thus you may understand why the theories were so long neglected. Even now, after having given some thought to the matter, I hesitate to term the thoughts I'm about to express "theories". I'd rather call them experiences and resultant conclusions.

The major problem confronting one who sets out to score for an orchestra is that of presenting the music most effectively. For the solution of this problem, three factors are absolutely essential: clarity, balance and a tasteful variety of tone color.

Clarity is the quality that tends to make every effect clear and each voice proportionately distinct. In order to acquire this quality it is necessary to refrain from over-orchestrating. I use the term "over-orchestrating" to define the excessive use of embellishments, ornate accompaniments and masses of sound. Very often, one who scores is tempted to indulge in such excesses, perhaps due to his desire to avoid thinness. Thinness should indeed be avoided, but not by going to a worse extreme. Such excesses may also be due to the pleasing effect an elaborate, over-orchestrated score has on the eye. It is true that a score of this sort displays visual evidence of skill. But one must not for a moment lose sight of the fact that the message of music can be comprehended only by man's aural sense. A florid orchestration is generally thick and indefinite; masses of sound always confuse the ear.

If one employs a contrapuntal style it is best for the sake of clarity that he limit the number of counterpoints. The rather simple combination of a melody with one striking counter-theme against an appropriate background will often be more pleasing than the more complicated contrapuntal treatments. I don't mean to give the impression that I believe such a limitation as that just cited should be strictly observed. Use as many counter-themes as may be effectively employed, but dovetail them in such a manner that each will stand out distinctly. Remember always the limitations of the ear!

Another thought of great importance in orchestrating is that the melody should always stand out prominently. All else that accompanies it should be subordinated to it, and constant caution must be exercised lest the melody be obscured by having too much going against it.

I've mentioned balance separately despite the fact that balance and clarity are related. Clarity depends to a large extent on balance, for a poorly balanced orchestration can never be clear. My reason for considering balance separately is that it lies principally in the sphere of physics, being gained by cold calculation more than through the artistic sensibilities. Undoubtedly, this is the reason it is so difficult to attain! Such a conclusion appears logical when we remember that the artistic mind is prone to shun cold reasoning. Balance can be a great problem to the beginner, but as experience broadens the difficulty lessens. In other words, proficiency in balancing instruments can be acquired only through experience. The first step toward the necessary experience should be to become intimately acquainted with each instrument: its dynamic possibilities as well as its tone quality in each register. With this knowledge, it is easier to reckon the effect of any combination of instruments and to distribute the voices so as to avoid having any stand out with undue prominence.

The third factor, a tasteful variety of tone color, is purely artistic in nature, and the extent to which it may be attained depends solely upon the degree of taste possessed by the arranger. Pleasing contrasts that bear some relation, one to the other, define "tasteful variety". Probably the first question that arises when one prepares to score is, "What color is best at this or that point?" This question shouldn't be settled at random. Neither should a passage be assigned to some instrument merely because it can be played easily upon that instrument. The desired mood should be considered first, and that mood should govern not only the choice of instruments for that passage but also the choice of color for the passage that follows. You will remember that my definition "tasteful variety" is "pleasing contrasts that are related". This relationship, then, should be one of mood.

At this point, I must stress the importance of choosing the instrument that will portray exactly the mood desired. I will also illustrate a variety of moods that may be obtained through assigning one passage, with unaltered accompaniment, to different instruments. Suppose we had a melody in the minor mode lying above a throbbing string accompaniment. Let us also suppose that the compass of this melody makes possible its performance upon flute, English horn, horn, or 'celli. (Remember that the string accompainment remains unaltered.) If we assign this melody to flute we gain the passive mood of tender longing. If we give it to English horn the resultant mood is one of melancholy. If we give it to horn it assumes an ominous aspect, especially if the horn be closed. If we have the 'celli sing it the effect is one of deep-seated grief that knows no repression. This illustration should serve to show the care that must be given to the choice of instruments.

I scarcely need to emphasize the necessity for contrasts, because we all know that man's craving for variety is inherent in his nature. Tone color *must* change, and it is important that the changes occur at the proper place. It is, of course, impossible to make any definite statement concerning the proper places for such changes as this depends upon the style of the music. There are times when it is advisable to give an entire passage to one instrument or choir. At other times it may be advisable to assign the first part of a passage to one instrument or group of instruments and the latter part to another instrument or group of instruments in a sort of antiphonal manner. And then the style of the music may call for more or less frequent changes. But no color should at any time be retained too long, for the most beautiful effect will become monotonous if it lasts overlong. It should be continued only long enough for the hearer to grasp its beauty. Then a new color should be introduced.

A nude style of orchestrating (i.e., one that leans not so far toward re-inforcing) is best suited for attaining variety of color. I don't mean to imply that re-inforcing should be avoided, for it has its uses and is particularly valuable when intensity is desired. But *restraint* in the practice of reinforcing will tend to heighten the brilliance of an orchestration, and to produce contrasts that are more striking.

Now, for some of the experiences and practices that have proved helpful to me personally. At the beginning it was, as may be expected, necessary for me to imitate. During my period of imitation, I learned two valuable lessons. The first: it's best for a beginner to choose as examples only the works of the best orchestrators.

The second: one shouldn't confine his imitation to the works of a single composer or orchestrator for, in so doing, he is likely to fall under an influence which will be hard to cast off later.

During my period of imitation, which was rather long lasting, I grasped every opportunity to become familiar with the various instruments, learned to play some of them, and jotted down in notebooks combinations of instruments which I thought might portray moods of all sorts. You would certainly be amused if you could see some of the impossible and far-fetched ideas my notebooks contained!

All the while I was drawing nearer the starting point—the period when one has gained enough experience for his own individuality to begin its development. That period finally came for me, heralded by an ungovernable impulse to combine instruments in many new ways. And then another lesson was learned: that some of the most striking effects are comparatively simple. Since then, I have learned many more lessons and have made many errors, but the more I progress the more convinced I am that a simple style of scoring achieves best results. In fact, the clearly defined effects which should be the aim of everyone who scores for orchestra can be obtained *only* through simplicity.

This has been particularly impressed upon me during the past year because of having been forced to adopt an altogether different style of orchestrating in order to get certain results with a limited group of players. This experience taught me how to employ individual instruments in a simple but effective manner, and caused me to believe that beauty can be expressed only in terms of simplicity.

Another valuable lesson I've learned is that one should never fail to give the members of the orchestra consideration. Indifferent playing will spoil the most beautiful passage, and unless the interest of the players is gained, their execution is apt to be more or less indifferent. Their interest can only be gained by giving them, whenever possible, something to play that they will enjoy playing.

Experience has also taught me that it doesn't always pay to accept statements regarding impossible orchestral combinations without first testing them and proving their value. Once I was told that a bass clarinet should never be combined with brass instruments. Later I discovered that there are ways in which they may be combined, and I was fortunate enough to gain a very pleasing effect by combining three muted trumpets, solo 'cello and bass clarinet.

On another occasion, it was said that celesta and chimes should never be combined. Yet a satisfactory pianissimo effect results from the combination of three clarinets playing sustained chords in the low register, chime struck lightly near where it is suspended with triangle beater, and celesta. A short interval between the chime stroke and the entry of the celesta is necessary.

There is one overall truth that I've learned. Probably it's best that I approach it by way of another truth. Although material means must be employed in the production of music, music is actually spiritual in nature, and its message is addressed to the soul. I became aware of this truth long ago, together with the other truth that goes hand in hand with it. That is that the voice of inspiration is the voice of God, and the soul of man must first hear it before its message may be transferred to the intellect. Anyone who wishes to hear the voice of inspiration clearly must be in accord with its possessor, and he may attain this accord through prayer.

Before beginning to work on any musical problem, I pray. And my prayers are always answered.

W. G. S.

Today, there seems to be varying ideas as to just what a composer is. Some people think that anyone who writes a song is a composer; others think that anyone who arranges a Spiritual is a composer. My own view is that a real composer should be one whose studies in many fields, added to his natural talent, enable him to try, at last, to walk in the paths of those master musicians who wrote in larger forms: symphonies, operas, chamber music, and so on. Of course, writing songs and arranging Spirituals do call for many of the abilities of a real composer, and many composers do make excursions into those realms, with great success. In other words, a composer can write songs or make arrangements, but not every arranger or songwriter can be a composer.

It is for this reason that I would like to consider first the qualities a composer must have, then to tell you of my own approach to a new composition and of the steps taken in building the composition from its inception, illustrating this with excerpts from my *Afro-American Symphony*.

What are the qualities which must be inherent in the person who aspires to write music? First, and most important, is the ability to induce the flow of inspiration, that indefinable element which transforms lifeless intervals into throbbing, vital and heart-warming music. Brahms looked on it as a spiritual communion. Wagner also realized its importance. Experience has taught me that the ability to induce the flow of inspiration is of the greatest importance, for without it one's efforts often have little value. There is a spontaneous kind of inspiration that comes of its own accord and, more often, an effort must be made to contact it and that can be very painful. Many composers keep notebooks of themes that have come to them spontaneously and refer to them when they need thematic material for a new work. This is a helpful practice.

Very often I have had the experience (as I understand many writers and other composers have had) of getting a theme after I've gone to bed at night. At such times it is always difficult to retain it long enough to put it on paper, so I developed the habit of visualizing it and thus helping to keep it in my memory until I could get to my notebook, usually in the following morning, and recording it for future use. It has sometimes been my feeling that I have heard such themes with the inner ear, a sort of psychic process.

One of the results of being able to tap the fount of inspiration is a melodic gift, and I cannot emphasize too much the importance of this gift, which seems to be so woefully lacking in so many contemporary composers. The so-called "creators" who lack the gift of melody always direct their messages to the intellect rather than to the heart, or soul—and this explains the dry, boring music they turn out.

Probably next in importance is a well-developed sense of proportion. Whether the listener is aware of it or not, the form (or architecture) of a composition can do a great deal to help or hinder his enjoyment. Poor form may produce a fragmentary, lopsided or insufficiently balanced piece of music, whereas hearing a well-formed musical work gives as much satisfaction as that derived from seeing an artistically designed building. In fact, in one way or another, form plays an outstanding role in all of the arts. Most people, even when they do not think of it in technical terms, are intuitively aware of it, or of its lack, when hearing music, or viewing works of art.

All of us have heard music which seems to be so lacking in contrast that it becomes boring. The only way this can be avoided is for a composer to be gifted with inventive ability. In order to sustain the listener's interest, the themes of a piece of music must undergo changes in rhythm, harmony, melody, and so forth—all of these changes being dominated by the musical intellect so that there is an effect of unity without undue repetition.

Now let's explore the approach to the creation of a new piece of music. The first step is to obtain thematic material and, if the composer has followed the practice of keeping a notebook such as I mentioned earlier, he may find satisfactory themes in this. If he doesn't, he must rely on the inspiration of the moment to produce what he needs. I prefer to do this after retiring at night and just before falling off to sleep. The following day, I decide on the way in which the thematic material will be presented.

Once having decided on which themes to use, I then go to planning the form of the new composition. My usual practice is to map out a plan which conforms loosely to the established rules of musical form, and then deviate from it as I see fit. This method

109

serves as a stimulant to invention and inspiration.

It goes without saying that the harmonic pattern of the Principal Theme will influence the overall harmonic treatment of a movement, yet the composer doesn't have to limit himself to that particular harmonic idiom. As his work progresses, new ideas will develop that will fit harmoniously into the general pattern. If one works at a rate of speed which allows him to understand his own material better, it will unfold itself in such a way as to seem to dictate its own treatment. This conforms to what some playwrights have said of their work: that as their characters grow within the framework of the drama, they often seem to dictate their own speech, actions, and even the direction of the plot.

After the preliminary period of planning and the initial creative steps have been taken, the composer may begin the sketch of his composition. This rough draft always undergoes numerous changes as it grows. Some composers wait until they are satisfied with the sketch before planning the orchestration. I don't, because I generally compose directly for orchestra. In other words, as each idea comes, I hear it orchestrally, and my notations for the orchestra score are written into my sketches. But before turning to the actual writing of the orchestration there is the additional task of testing and polishing what has been written. This includes a thorough examination of the music in order to determine nuances, tempi, phrasing, and so on.

Next comes the writing of the orchestra score, which is followed by the extracting of the parts. Many composers consider this a chore and try in every possible way to get out of it—some assigning it to their pupils and some asking for funds to employ professional copyists. I, however, gladly do my own copying since it gives me a pleasant way to read proof on the orchestra score. This is the final step, provided that the music proves to be satisfactory when it is performed. If it is not, then revisions are necessary.

Incidentally, all of the music following the sketch is written on onion skin, or transparent reproducing paper from which any number of copies can be made, thus reducing the cost of providing all the copies needed for an orchestral performance. Before leaving this aspect of the composing process, I would like to stress the necessity for legibility. The initial sketch may be as haphazard as the composer wishes as long as he can read it—because he is the only person who has to deal with it. But everything that follows must be done with the greatest of care, for if the musicians cannot read the music well, they will inevitably make mistakes and this leads to a useless waste of rehearsal time, and could also result in a bad performance.

Now, to demonstrate the progress of a composition after the first steps of planning, I will use brief extracts from the *Afro-American Symphony*. Long before writing this Symphony I had recognized the musical value of the Blues and had decided to use a theme in the Blues idiom as the basis for a major symphonic composition. When I was ready to launch this project I did not want to use a theme some folk singer had already created, but decided to create my own theme in the Blues idiom.

W. G. S.

AN AFRO-AMERICAN COMPOSER'S VIEWPOINT

Melody, in my opinion, is the most important musical element. After melody comes harmony; then form, rhythm, and dynamics. I prefer music that suggests a program to either pure or program music in the strict sense. I find mechanically produced music valuable as a means of study; but even at its best it fails to satisfy me completely. My greatest enjoyment in a musical performance comes through seeing as well as hearing the artist.

The exotic in music is certainly desirable, but if one loses sight of the conventional in seeking for strange effects, the results are almost certain to be so extreme as to confound the faculties of the listeners. Still, composers should never confine themselves to materials already invented, and I do not believe that any one tonality is of itself more significant than another. I am unable to understand how one can rely solely on feeling when composing. The tongue can utter the letters of the alphabet, but it is the intellect alone that makes it possible to combine them so as to form words. Likewise a fragment of a musical composition may be conceived through inspiration or feeling, but its development lies altogether within the realm of intellect.

Colored people in America have a natural and deep-rooted feeling for music, for melody, harmony, and rhythm. Our music possesses exoticism without straining for strangeness. The natural practices in this music open up a new field which can be of value in larger musical works when constructed into organized form by a composer who, having the underlying feeling, develops it through his intellect.

W. G. S.

HORIZONS UNLIMITED

W e live in a country where men are free to express themselves as they wish in every field of endeavor, particularly in the arts. And yet, despite this freedom, some of us in the creative field of music find ourselves apparently with our horizons limited. This cannot be a limitation placed on us by outsiders—though their opinions may certainly have something to do with influencing us. Instead, it is a limitation that some of us have placed on ourselves, thinking perhaps that it will please outsiders.

In hearing the work of many young composers lately, I've been astonished to see how much of it follows a pattern. Now, I don't disagree totally with that pattern. I simply don't see how it's possible for so many to fall into it and still retain their identities as individuals.

There are people who seem to have decided that a certain type of music is the only acceptable music for our modern times. There are musicians who seem to feel it necessary for *all* to compose that type of music, just as so many novelists feel it necessary to write brutally realistic books in order to succeed. There is a tendency in all the arts toward the new, the sensational, the cerebral, rather than the beautiful and the worthwhile. It's important to have the new, sensational products, but it's important to have beauty too. How can we afford to emphasize one more than the other?

First of all, I don't think that it is good for the world of music to have everything come out of the same mold. God didn't place only roses on earth, or only lilies or only violets. He put flowers of many sorts and many colors here, the beauty of each enhancing that of the others. Anyone who underestimates the great value of differences would do well to remember that life would indeed be dull without variety. Progress would be impossible if all thought alike. It follows, then, that everyone should work toward variety, each individual expressing himself, particularly if he has decided to enter the creative field. He should begin by analyzing himself and his capabilities, in order to learn whether he is really doing —or will be doing—what he *really* wants to do.

Supposing someone has an inclination to write in the traditional style. Should he let someone else talk him out of it? By all means, no. Nor should he allow himself to be persuaded to drop the so-called "ultra-modern" style, if he honestly feels inclined toward that. I stress the word "honestly" here, because (as I said before) I sometimes wonder how many of the people who write in that style do so out of a sense of deep conviction, and how many of them are simply agreeing with the fad of the moment. At any rate, a composer should follow his own leanings. If all composers would do that, and would develop their own capabilities to the best of their ability, we would soon have an infinite variety and a host of new colors in the music now being composed.

I speak as a composer who has, in a very real sense, been through the mill. In my early days, I studied at Conservatories with Conservatory-trained teachers. There I learned the traditions of music and acquired the basic tools of the trade. If I had stopped there, the sort of music I later composed might have been quite different. But necessity forced me to earn a living, so I turned to the field of commercial music.

Back in the days when America became aware of the "Blues", I worked with W. C. Handy in his office on Beale Street in Memphis. This certainly would not seem to be an occupation nor a place where anything of real musical value could be gained. Nor would nearby Gayoso Street, which was then a somewhat disreputable section. But, in searching for musical experiences that might later help me, I found there an undeniable color and a musical atmosphere that stemmed directly from the folk.

Any alert musician could learn something, even in that sordid atmosphere. W. C. Handy listened and learned—and what he learned profitted him financially and in other ways in the succeeding years. He, of course, belongs in the popular field of music. But if a popular composer could profit by such contacts with folk music, why couldn't a serious composer? Instead of having a feeling of condescension, I tried to keep my ears open so that I could absorb and make mental notes of things that might be valuable later.

As the years went on, and I went from one commercial job to another, there were always people who tried to make me believe that the commercial field was an end in itself, and who argued that I should not waste my time on what is now often called "long-hair" music. In this, I disagreed. I felt that I was learning something valuable, but only insofar as I could use it to serve a larger purpose.

114

The next important step was my study with Edgar Varese. He might be classed as one of the most extreme of the ultramodernists. He took for himself, and encouraged in others, absolute freedom in composing. Inevitably, while I was studying with him, I began to think as he did and to compose music which was performed; music which was applauded by the avant-garde, such as were found in the International Composers' Guild. As a matter of fact, I was so intrigued by what I learned from Mr. Varese that I let it get the better of me. I became its servant, not its master. It followed as a matter of course that, after freeing me from the limitation of tradition, it too began to limit me.

It took me a little while to realize that it *was* limiting me, and that the ultra-modern style alone (that is to say, in its unmodified form) did not allow me to express myself as I wished. I sought then to develop a style that debarred neither the ultra-modern nor the conventional.

Certain people thought this decision was unwise, and tried to persuade me to stay strictly in the ultra-modern fold. I didn't do it, but at the same time, the things I learned from Mr. Varese—let us call them the horizons he opened up to me—have had a profound effect on the music I have written since then. The experience I gained was thus most valuable even thought it did not have the result that might have been expected.

After this period, I felt that I wanted for a while to devote myself to writing racial music. And here, because of my own racial background, a great many people decided that I ought to confine myself to that sort of music. In that too, I disagreed. I was glad to write Negro music then, and I still do it when I feel so inclined, for I have a great love and respect for the idiom. But it has certainly not been the *only* musical idiom to attract me.

Fortunately for me, nobody tried to talk me out of the two things that strikingly influenced my musical learnings, possibly because those influences were not the sort which make themselves known to outsiders as readily as others. The first was my love for grand opera, born around 1911 when my stepfather bought many of the early Red Seal recordings for our home record library. I knew then that I would be happy only if someday I could compose operatic music, and I have definitely leaned toward a lyric style for that reason.

The second influence had to do with writing for the symphony orchestra, something which has deeply interested me from the very start of my musical life. Many years ago, I began to evolve theories pertaining to orchestration, and to experiment with them from time to time. Applying those theories has tended to modify, perhaps even to curtail, the development of a contrapuntal style as it is known today. However, their use has enabled me to better achieve the result I sought.

Today the music I write stems in some degree from all of my experiences, but it is what *I* would like to write, not what others have insisted that I write. Some people have been kind enough to say that I have developed a distinctly personal style of musical expression. I hope they are right, and if they are, I'm sure it has come from keeping an open mind, meanwhile making an effort to select what is valuable and to reject what is unimportant, in my estimation.

Ask yourselves, for instance: what would Wagner have become if he had been willing to mold himself to suit the whims and tastes of the critic Hanslick? What would have happened to Puccini had he allowed himself to follow the dictates of the critics who wrote so unkindly of his work?

In this respect, may I say that no one on earth, be he musician or critic, has the right to decide arbitrarily what form music shall take and to renounce what doesn't conform to his dictum. I recall a music-lover who heard a new work by Stravinsky and did not like it. In commenting on it, he said, "If this is the direction *music* is going to take, I do not approve." I believe that Stravinsky himself would be the last person to feel that *music* had to take a certain direction just because he composed in a particular way. He, as a creator, has always composed according to his own artistic conscience. If the general trend of music follows him, it is not—to the best of my belief—because he has consciously tried to force it.

It was, I believe, the critic Olin Downes who long ago made up his mind that the great American opera would have to come from a composer belonging to the field of American light opera, or the field of musical comedy. His reasons for thinking so may have been very good indeed, but how could he, or anyone else, possibly anticipate what might come from a creative mind in the future? If he had been living in Bach's time, could he have anticipated Beethoven? Or, in the time of Pergolesi, would anyone have an-

116

ticipated Verdi? That being the case, Mr. Downes shouldn't have presumed to limit in advance the direction American opera should or would take.

People who assert that *their* way is the *only* way retard progress. They aren't wise enough, or just enough, to realize that even though they may be at variance with a school of thought, that school of thought must not be denied the right to express, for it too must contain elements of truth, just as everything contains elements of truth. Probably the acid test of a composer's right to wear the mantle of freedom is his willingness to accord others the same rights that he enjoys.

There is someone else who has the right to freedom where music is concerned. That someone is usually the last to be considered, but the most important of all, namely: the audience. Remember, just because you write something and you hope the audience will like it, the audience doesn't have to do so, and if it doesn't, that is the privilege of each individual listener. A composer's failure to consider the audience is an abuse of his own freedom.

One very well-known contemporary composer has been threatening lately that music will come to a dead end if audiences and performers refuse to give consideration to the type of music he and others like him are turning out. I don't think that will be true at all. In my opinion, and in the opinion of composer George Frederick McKay, audiences are more astute in the aggregate than most people imagine. And it is my feeling that their *spontaneous* response should be the strongest influence on a composer.

Now, this should not be a limitation for the composer; it should be a challenge. To be able to reach an audience without "writing down" and without becoming cheap should be the goal of everyone in the creative field, for a composer fails to do his duty to the development of music when he writes down to his hearers, nor does he edify, uplift, please or compliment those hearers when he does so. Just as every new doctor takes the Hippocratic oath, so should everyone who undertakes the job of composing music realize that it means a life of service.

American industry should have proved to all of us that *everything is*, or should be, created to fill a human need. Music is no exception to this rule. If the composer expects to have his music performed for people, he must give those people something they want and need. If he does not, then he had better not have his music played in public at all. He might just as well isolate himself in an ivory tower where he can compose for himself alone. When an industrial plant finds that one of its products has not succeeded in serving the public, it discontinues that product, even though its manufacturers may reserve the right to disagree with the public's verdict.

In other words, music shouldn't only appeal to the vanity of the person who writes it. It should serve others just as religion serves mankind, by helping people to live better lives and by giving them —even if only for an instant—a glimpse of real inspiration. And, if we want music to appeal to more people we must address our message to the heart as well as to the intellect. In trying to understand the needs of others a whole new world will open to us.

There are always the scoffers who will insist that a composer who writes within his audience's reach is "popular". Well, Christ spoke in simple, easily-understood terms that everyone could understand. His message has proved to be popular throughout the ages—but not the sort of "popularity" implied by people who scorn the easly-understood composer. To be understood as Christ is understood, one's message must be clear, satisfying and important.

A further sidelight on those scoffers who lightly use the word "popular": they are, I think, the first to be delighted when audiences approve their work, and the first to have their feelings hurt when audiences don't understand them. I recall only too well some composers in particular, many years ago, who smugly turned up their noses at Puccini. In all the intervening years, they haven't turned out a single work that could approach Puccini's in inspiration, even though they have tried. I wonder if they, in secret, do not envy the qualities they profess to scorn.

Let's return momentarily to listeners. One thing I will say about the American audience: in the past it has been willing to listen to something new. The audiences for Dr. Hanson's American Composers' Concerts in Rochester performed a great service for native composers by that willingness; the same may be said of the audiences who came to concerts of the International Composers' Guild in New York's old Aeolian Hall. They provided sharp and immediate reactions: sometimes approval, sometimes disapproval. As the years went on and the music that was offered continued to be, in a large degree, the same sort of music which had been disapproved, the audiences lost much of their early interest, and even lost the energy to hiss and protest. They simply turned the dials when it was broadcast, or just didn't pay admission to attend the concerts at which it was performed.

In accepting the verdict of the public, however, the composer ought always to be analytical. He should be sure that it *is* public opinion that speaks, rather than the opinion of a few people who hope to trick the masses into accepting *their* beliefs. In my case, the people who sought to exert influence belonged to small groups; the general public's verdict was often quite different from theirs. When such individuals or small groups start to try to persuade creators to come around to their viewpoints, they invariably try to induce a fear of being called "unsophisticated", "old-fashioned", or "ignorant". It's sometimes very difficult to be immune to such pressure, because no one likes to feel that he is ignorant, old-fashioned or unsophisticated. But it's always possible to recognize these things for what they really are: just taunts, and so to resist them.

Only the intellectual coward fails to analyze such terms and to accept them at their face value, which is the simple need for some individuals (usually those who are not capable of creating on their own) to feel that they have gained power or influence over some other individual.

With that in mind, I think it would be interesting now to consider some of the musical terms that are used while people are trying to persuade other people to one view or the other. The first one might be the word, "contemporary". This has often been mis-used as far as music is concerned. For example, some years ago, a New York composer made a trip to Southern California and, while here, heard some of a West Coast ultra-modernist's new compositions. He said, according to report, that he was astonished that the Westerner could live 'way out here in California and yet write music that is just as "contemporary" as the music being composed in the East.

Now, quite aside from the wisdom of believing that a composer has to live in a particular place to be able to write a particular sort of music, I would also question the Easterner's use of the word "contemporary" in this respect. As a matter of plain fact, the music I write, the music you write, or that written by any other living composer is "contemporary" music, no matter what the style of its

119

composition, because we are living at the present time which, according to my dictionary, means a contemporary time. So, if the Eastern composer was implying that only one type of composing can be considered contemporary, I think he was limiting his own thinking.

Next, the terms "idiom" and "style". These are often heard nowadays, and are sometimes used interchangeably. I myself have been guilty of using them interchangeably, when my speech runs too quickly ahead of my thoughts. These terms probably came to be applied to music *after* the period when compositions generally conformed to traditional patterns. As more and more composers broke with the past, they were said to be writing in certain idioms. In my view, an idiom is something that pertains to groups of people. As you well know, we have in the United States a great many idioms, some aboriginal, some springing from the people who came here from other lands. Someday probably the separate idioms in America may merge, or a composer will come along who will make an overall use of them and we will then have a distinctly native idiom, recognizable as such.

Undoubtedly the music which exemplifies a folk idiom was originally created by individuals, now nameless, but over a period of years, the people in general have accepted it as their own, often adding to it with the passage of time, so that it now speaks for *people*, rather than for individual creators.

Because an idiom stems from, and belongs to, the people, a composer who belongs to a particular group of people may have musical tendencies expressive of his people's idiom. He may consciously study that idiom and employ its characteristics, or he may simply write music, unconsciously expressing his heritage. In any event, "idiom" is rarely something that can be acquired or discarded at will. It should be an integral part of every composer, to such an extent that no one could argue him out of it even if he tried. There have been instances where composers have adopted, for specific purposes, the idioms of people foreign to them. Their successes or failures have been due entirely to the degree of their own sensitivity and adaptability.

A good example of the manner in which a composer can be influenced by a racial idiom and yet be able to develope an individual style is expressed in this obituary, written in Australia after the death of Sibelius: "It has been said that the art of Sibelius took

120

its root in the soil of his country, but became individualized by contact with his experience of life. Thus, because of his strong personal bias, combined with his racial consciousness, he evolved an artistic code of his own, neither modern nor archaic; his music is simply unlike any other."

"Style" is quite a different matter. It is a personal thing dictated largely by personal taste and, because of that, can be shaped by the individual's conscious mind. In other words, a style can be acquired, and an idiom can play a part in influencing that style.

Nowadays, there are two common concepts of style. One is not far removed from conventional music. The other departs radically from what we have known in the past. I long ago decided not to limit myself to the ultra-modern style, but I have never failed to perceive its value, or to use it whenever its use seemed to be justified. That being the case, I don't criticize either mode of expression —I take issue only with those people who espouse one or the other style and refuse to accept or approve any other. They are comparable to a painter who decides to use only the cool colors, or vice versa.

Some people scorn consonance in writing contemporary music, yet loudly praise Bach and other classicists. This appears inconsistent and hypocritical to me. If they really like the old masters so well, why can't they enjoy a tonic triad when it appears in the music of today?

On the other hand, there are those who close their minds to even the slightest departures from consonance. These extremists also display a lack of balance.

Additionally, there are other elements in the music of today which, in my opinion, deserve discussion and clarification. For one instance, the matter of *tonality*. Absence of tonality distresses me, producing a feeling of having lost my sense of direction and struggling to re-orientate myself.

And then, *harmony* which means, according to Webster, an agreeable blending of tones. Probably there are some who are not too greatly concerned over it, while others may give it undue importance. Unfortunately, many claim that harmonic resources have been exhausted, so they have turned to cacophony. I have the feeling that earnest experimentation, unhampered by the restrictions imposed by isms, should reveal that there is much more to be discovered in this field.

There is very little to be said concerning the *counterpoint* of to-day other than that some composers seem to be so greatly absorbed in directing the horizontal progress of the various voices that the vertical results of this same progress are neglected. Incidentally, when counterpoint calls attention to itself, crying out loudly, "Listen to me! I'm counterpoint, and I'm important", then it isn't good counterpoint.

Rhythm is so often taken for granted that it is sometimes hard to realize that some composers don't consider it important—at least, in a recognizable form. One of my colleagues once remarked that there is a difference of opinion as to what constitutes a rhythm, and then he cited a rhythm so stagnant that it approached actual inertia. Though the example he offered was indeed a rhythm in the broadest sense of the word, it had little value. Any rhythm worthy of the name should be recognizable as such even by laymen. Incidentally, this is a field that composers would do well to explore further. Someone may discover eventually that there is such a thing as rhythmic counterpoint, if that discovery has not already been made.

Last of all, there is *inspiration*. How very important it is! True, the mechanical side of creative work is important, but it should never take the precedence over inspiration.

All of these elements are vital to the development of the well-rounded composer, who cannot afford to exclude *anything* that may be useful to him. In this connection, let me make a qualifying statement. In advocating the study and use of all available materials, all idioms, all traditions and all forms of musical expression, I am decidedly *not* endorsing the creation of musical hodge-podges. It would be wrong to construct compositions in which a conscious effort is made to employ a variety of styles. It would be equally wrong for us to deny ourselves the right to use a contrasting style when it seems to be needed, and the biggest mistake of all would be to deny ourselves the right to learn all there is to know about *all* musical elements available to us.

No, my suggestion is that everyone would profit by being able to know and use various styles if and when he wishes. Then, the innate character of each composition will itself dictate the treatment, the style and the form the music is going to take. No outsider should presume to tamper with a composer's conviction in that respect. No matter how sensitive and alert we are to outside influences, we should never allow them to throw us off balance. Criticism must be *evaluated* before it's accepted or rejected.

By all means, the young composer should learn from everything and everyone. He should realize that nothing is valueless or totally undesirable. He should listen to all his teachers, study his textbooks, absorb all the musical influences around him—but at the same time, reserve the right to disagree with anything he feels unable to accept.

There is no substitute for keeping an open mind and for analyzing both sides of a question. There is also no substitute for having the courage of one's convictions. No one really wants to be a carbon copy of anyone else, no matter how much he may admire the other person or his work.

I have always felt, when people have asked me to bow to their will, that I may indeed be wrong—but if I *am* wrong, let it be my own mistake, not one I have been led into. It may be that I am mistaken in having tried to establish my own mode of musical expression. But it more nearly expresses my true self than any mode I might have borrowed! In it I have sought to attain a degree of balance in the use of both dissonance and consonance, remembering that while the music that leans toward the dissonant style expands the musical horizon and is unquestionably an asset, it is not in itself the only, or the most desirable end—remembering too that consonance will never be outmoded.

Beethoven was said to have "freed" music because he had courage enough to investigate new horizons. Yet he did not discard what had gone before!

Our world is big enough for every idea. In it we all can enjoy freedom. Let us then develop in ourselves those qualities that will enable us to use these ideas and this freedom in opening the new horizons which *always* exist—only waiting for the magic touch of inspiration to release them for mankind.

W. G. S.

A COMPOSER'S VIEWPOINT

I would like to preface my remarks by stating what will soon be an obvious fact to all of you, namely that I am a composer, and not an orator. You may well decide that composers such as I ought to devote themselves to composing, not talking. However, I have been asked to speak in public so often in recent years that I have tried to accustom myself to what is expected, and I ask you to bear with me now through my ordeal.

Furthermore, although we are committed to an extensive discussion of Black music, I would like to emphasize that I speak not only as a Negro, but also as an American. For a long time we Afro-Americans needed something like the fact that Black can be beautiful to give us identity and pride in our racial heritage. Now that has been accomplished. Most of us have come to realize that Black is indeed beautiful, but only as White, Brown, or Yellow are beautiful: when we make it so. The term has served its purpose, so I hope from this time forward we will all want to emphasize our American ties, as well as our African heritage. Our parents and grandparents, I think, wanted us above all else to be good Americans and to get a substantial education, so that we could compete on an equal basis with all other Americans. And speaking about parents and grandparents, let's recapitulate for a few minutes and recall what it was like to be a Negro musician then, and how far we have progressed. Looking at the past may shed some light on the future.

To begin with, my father was one of those who endured all sorts of sacrifices in order to get an education and to become, on the side, a musician. Long before the turn of the century, he worked hard toward this end. He taught mathematics, had a half interest in a store, sang solos in church, and learned to play the cornet the hard way. Each lesson cost him a seventy-five mile trip from Woodville, Mississippi, to Baton Rouge, Louisiana, where the only competent teacher for miles around could be found. When he had absorbed enough of this training, he formed the only brass band in Woodville. People who knew him in those days said that he was admired by both Negroes and Whites. I can well believe it, for many Southern people have a feeling of genuine affection for

124

Negro musicians—not enough, of course, to make them acceptable as equals, but enough to make them the objects of a certain amount of indulgence. W. C. Handy once elaborated on this by saying that if he needed money, he could get it if he pretended he wanted it to buy liquor or to gamble, but not if he said he wanted it to buy books for his children. I think this affection for Negro musicians has extended to the present day, when so many Southerners are truly interested in culture, and so many take pride in those Negro artists who have succeeded and who had their roots in the South.

My father may have been, as they said, the idol of the town, but he surely would have found it difficult to transform that worship into cash at that time and in that area. In fact, I wonder whether he ever was paid at all for his musical activities. Had he lived beyond his twenty-fourth year, he might have had enough drive to earn his living in music if he chose to do so, for he was an ambitious young man. But he didn't live, so we'll never know.

The earning capacity of Negro musicians was indeed limited in those days, and continued to be so for quite a while. I recall the serenaders, small groups of Negro musicians who, when I was a boy, would go from house to house at night, playing stringed instruments and singing. Residents would throw them coins. Yesterday that was a fitting reward. Today it would be less than a mere pittance.

When I was along in my school years, my mother engaged a teacher to give me violin lessons, and encouraged me to study music. However, I didn't want to be a performer. I wanted to compose, and no sooner did I learn to read music than I wanted to write it. This was fine, as far as my mother was concerned, until she learned that I wanted to make music my life's work. Then she opposed me. This seemed strange to me at the time, because my mother was herself a person of more than ordinary artistic ability. She taught English in the secondary school, wrote and directed plays, painted, and played the piano a little. Her own goals were high. She constantly urged me to make something of myself, and not to follow the path of least resistance. However, a career in music was outside the bounds of consideration for her and, as she persisted in her efforts to discourage me, I began to understand why. The Negro musicians of her day were not socially accepted into the better Negro homes. In fact, many Colored people considered them immoral. They disapproved of their drinking, and they certainly looked down on their earning capacity! My mother was very explicit on the latter count. She pictured me as wearing threadbare clothes, starving, and unable to provide the bare necessities of life. Her ridicule was fairly constant and unwavering. She wanted me to become a doctor so I could make enough money to live on. Today I can see that she did what she did for my benefit, yet even today it is hard for me to realize that the structure of Negro society at that time was such that even a woman of her vision could not understand that the kind of composer I meant to be was far different from her concept, nor would she or others of that period have envisioned an Afro-American attaining a position of prominence in the symphonic or operatic fields! You can understand that when I tell you that not until I got to Oberlin and had reached my majority did I ever hear a symphony orchestra! That would explain it. I wonder what the people of that day would say today, when so many American Negroes are seeking to reach such goals, with a reasonable number actually making the grade.

After I left college, economic and racial factors did indeed influence my way of life—to my ultimate advantage, however. I was determined to make a living in music, and the popular field was the only commercial field open to me and others like me. I went into it with one thought uppermost in my mind: I intended to learn all I could from American popular music in order to put the knowledge to good use in my later career. In other words, I wanted to learn but not to make the popular field an end in itself. I still feel that this was a wise course of action, for what I learned there was not available anywhere else. It later balanced my conservatory training to give more facets to my musical personality.

When I went to work with W. C. Handy in Memphis in 1916, playing in his orchestra and arranging, I gained a first-hand contact with Negro folk music that was not available to me at home. I learned, for example, to appreciate the beauty of the blues, and to consider this the musical expression of the yearnings of a lowly people, instead of accepting it superfically as being immoral and sexy, as so many other people did.

Most of you are no doubt aware that there came a time in our musical history when American Negroes even looked down on spirituals, because they associated them with the days of slavery. Knowing this, you can well imagine the prejudice that existed against the blues which stemmed, supposedly, from the big city

126

dives. I recall when I was a boy in Little Rock asking a pianist to play the *Memphis Blues* for me. She was afraid, because of the bad reputation of the music. Fortunately, both spirituals and blues have emerged from the period of ill repute, and are now generally recognized as very important contributions of the Negro to our American life.

Other aspects of my association with Handy will shed light on the social conditions of the Negro musician of that period. At home I had been sheltered, and had moved in what I would consider enlightened social circles, but on the road with Handy and his orchestra, I found that the indulgence many people felt for Negro musicians did not extend to giving them much consideration for their ordinary needs. Handy's orchestra played the length and breadth of the South. Larger cities had accommodations for us (segregated, of course) but in some of the smaller communities there were no places for Negroes to stay. I remember once in winter, in the mountainous section not far from Bristol, Tennessee (where we were playing) we stayed in a mountain home where the flooring consisted of rough pieces of wood and the openings were almost a half inch apart. The wind blew through these openings, just as if we were outdoors. It was cold even in bed! And we had to eat grits and sow belly. I'll never forget that experience.

At another time, we were playing in a little town in Arkansas. It was very interesting there. A White man came and sat by me. He liked the 'cello, and he stayed right there and listened. He didn't get far away at all until it came time for us to quit playing. Handy went to collect his pay, which was given without question, but we discovered that no one had thought to make arrangements for our housing. There simply was no place to stay, so we walked back to the station. It was locked, and we were out in the cold. Handy took his cornet case, broke a window, and unlatched the door. We sat inside the station for the rest of the night, and Handy later paid for the broken window.

Our traveling was done in Jim Crow cars, which were usually only half cars. They offered very little that was comfortable or desirable: cinders, smoke, unpleasant odors, and the feeling of humiliation, being compelled to pay first-class fare for third-rate accommodations. One time in Alabama, a Negro prisoner was placed in our car. His captors relieved themselves of responsibility by locking him in the toilet which, by the way, was the only one on

127

the train Negro passengers could use. Under these circumstances, we naturally could not use it, but the prisoner solved our problem by breaking the window and escaping.

Early one morning, our train made a short stop in Rome, Georgia. We had gone all night without food, and we were all hungry. Again there was no place for us to eat. We were told at one restaurant that if we went to the back, we would be served. We didn't want to do that, partly because of the humiliation, and partly because we were afraid of missing the train, so we got back on and rode until past noon without food.

My last incident has a brighter ending. One day in a Kentucky town, we went to the Negro restaurant, but it smelled like a privy. None of us wanted to eat there, so we went to a White restaurant right in town, across from the old court house. We described our predicament to the owner and he promptly invited us in, sat us by the front window, and served us a delicious meal. With our thoughts geared to the reality of segregation, we had expected him to put up a screen in front of us, but he didn't. He treated us just like his other customers.

In relating this, I've had another purpose in mind besides telling you about Negro musicians and their world over a half-century ago. I have heard reports of Negroes today who are trying to turn the clock back, and bring separation and segregation again into our lives. I say they can't know what they are talking about. They have certainly never experienced segregation and its inconveniences as some of us have. Even if they do understand what it is, and are willing to endure its humiliations for themselves, it is not fair to advocate it for the rest of us and for our children. Instead of all this big separatist talk, they should get down on their knees and thank God that the present laws in the United States have made segregation illegal.

One prominent White California educator, on reviewing the current separatist efforts, recently wrote: "Shades of the Ku Klux Klan! What ever happened to the wonderful idea of America as one united people, the great melting pot of all nations, all colors, and all races? Has it gone forever down the drain of history? All of us had better hope not." Make no mistake about it, segregation today is illegal because those of us who came before fought a legal battle against it, and struggled against it in our rights as American citizens. And this was during a period when our opportunities were

128

so far less than those of today. We didn't waste any time and energy in returning hatred for hatred. Instead, we continued moving toward our goal, never forgetting that our progress was being hastened because of the help given us by many fine White Americans. We won the battle with their help. Now let's take a brief look at some of the conditions that existed before the battle was won.

Today there are several capable Negro orchestral conductors active in various parts of the world. But who remembers Alli Ross? He was a capable conductor in New York, not too long ago, who worked daily to prepare himself. Every morning he would have his coffee and toast, and then start reading scores. He couldn't get a real chance because of his color, and he died a frustrated man.

And when we look at the Negro players in some of our contemporary symphony orchestras, let's not forget the colored instrumentalists who tried so hard in the old days but were always rebuffed, and finally had to adopt different professions in order to make a living. By the time there came conductors and opportunities that would have given them a chance, they had grown rusty and could not qualify. But it was they, the seemingly unsuccessful, who by knocking at the doors so persistently, helped to open them for the Negro musicians who followed. We all owe them a great debt.[1]

Many of the pioneers of Negro music were contemporaries and close friends of mine. Each took a step toward the development of our racial culture and toward its integration into American culture. I never knew Samuel Coleridge-Taylor personally, but the very fact of his success as a serious composer served as an inspiration. In college, I even tried to make my hair grow like his. That was something of a task, because his hair was bushy, and mine was fairly straight.

I did know Harry T. Burleigh. He was such a gentleman; he had beautiful manners, courtly. I knew Nathaniel Dett, and Edmund Jenkins. Jenkins was a very talented young man, who died early. He had done some symphonic writing, and was working on a symphony when he died. Had he finished it, he would have been

---

[1] James Baldwin, in *The Fire Next Time* (Middlesex: Penquin Books, 1965, p. 85) states: "I have great respect for that unsung army of black men and women who trudged down back lanes and entered back doors, saying 'Yes, sir' and 'No, ma'am' in order to acquire a new roof for the schoolhouse, new chemistry lab, more beds for the dormitories, more dormitories."

the first. Clarence Cameron White, John Work, Florence Price—all of these are mentioned in Maud Cuney Hare's competently researched book, *Negro Musicians and Their Music.*

I also knew bandsmen like Frank Drye, instrumentalists like Joe Douglas, Louia Von Jones, and Hazel Harrison, singers like Sissieretta Jones (who was also known as the Black Patti), Roland Hayes and, later, Marian Anderson, as well as orchestrators like Will Vodery. All these and many others had individual contributions to make, and for none of them was the path unfailingly easy.

Credit has been given me for being the first Negro to conduct a major symphony orchestra in the United States, and the first to do the same in the Deep South, for being the first to write a symphony which was performed, the first to have an opera produced by a major American company, and first to conduct a White radio orchestra in New York. I would like to say here that none of these accomplishments would have been possible if it had not been for the work done before by so many of our pioneers—those who were successful in their respective fields, and those who were unsuccessful too. They made tremendous efforts in their lifetime, and thus made it easier for me and for the others who came after me. I cannot conceive of any possible way in which I or anyone else could have come up absolutely alone, without any predecessors, and could have made the grade, because I believe every accomplishment has to be built on foundations established long before.

I am so well aware of these past accomplishments that when I came across the book entitled *Black Music,* published in 1967 by a reputable New York firm, I was affronted when I glanced inside and found mention of only a few contemporary jazz artists, with not one acknowledgement of progress in any other field of Negro music. I ascribe this in some measure to a bias on the part of the writer, and in some measure to ignorance and bad taste, for although no one holds authentic jazz in higher esteem than I, I still refuse to concede that it is the only or even the most important form of Negro musical expression. True, it has spread all over the world, but so have Negro spirituals, and so, I venture to guess, would a certain amount of Negro symphonic music if it had behind it the same commercial drive that has long activated jazz.

I am equally affronted by what I have been told of the new courses in our universities, purporting to be courses in Negro music but actually no more than courses in jazz. If they are solely jazz courses, let them be so labelled. If they intend to be courses in Negro music, then let them encompass the whole panorama of Negro music: the study of the development of Negro music from the songs of the African natives, on to the classic period when Negro music was represented by men like Bridgetower (who was the first to perform Beethoven's *Kreutzer* sonata) and the Chevalier de Saint-Georges (an esteemed composer), even Beethoven (who some observers believe had Negro blood). From there the course could move on through the folk music of Latin America, the West Indies, the United States, and up to its individual creators and performers of today. What a fascinating area for research! It can't be dismissed lightly, but its true value can be assessed only in its relation to music as a whole and not a separate entity.

One of my friends, Theodore Phillips, who inaugurated and taught a course in Afro-American music at one of the Southern California colleges, now stresses the need for a formal study in depth, and insists that courses in Negro music should be a necessary part of the over-all study of music. Further, they should be made attractive to White as well as Colored students, for only in this way, he says, can Negro music be recognized for what it has already contributed to our culture, and I agree with this completely. It's my view that such a procedure would add a new dimension to our music, in that it would contribute to good public relations for the Negro, as it has so often in the past. Incidentally, in his initial days in the class, my friend was staggered to discover that only a few of his students had ever heard of a Negro spiritual, that none knew of the shouts or work songs! None were even aware of the advances in "serious" music!

Some of the students set themselves to challenging his every statement, no matter how simple or how obvious. Through the ages, students have been expected to inquire and to question. All of us have done it when we were forming our thoughts and planning our future actions. None of us accepted everything blindly. At the same time, it has generally been accepted that students are supposed to learn from their teachers, not to teach the teachers. It seems to me that our future might well depend on our willingness to receive instruction and to respect qualified instructors. No doubt some members of my friend's class shared the attitude of a seventeen-year-old Black Student Union member who was interviewed by the *Los Angeles Times* on March 14, 1969. He said that racist

131

training involved teaching about Johann Sebastian Bach, whom he described as "that old, dead punk." He added that he wanted to learn about Ray Charles, The Supremes, and about Black composers. From one of my personal experiences which I plan to recount later, I'm wondering if he really meant that, or if he only wanted to know about those who fitted neatly into his concepts.

In the first place, I would suggest that students who want to learn about Negro music should undertake it in all sincerity, not with the idea that they will be taking a snap course, or that they will be permitted to sit and listen to jazz recordings during every class period. This may be enjoyable, but it is not genuine study. The latter in my opinion should be historical, analytical, comparative, and should be undertaken above all with an open mind. It should be studied and explored in all seriousness, not merely as a means of getting credits without working for them. Along with this, the Negro student of music should learn about Bach, "that old, dead punk," and all the other composers who have made valuable contributions to music. He should prepare himself from all angles.

Now that the doors are opening to us, it would be tragic to have them shut in our faces again because those who enter are not yet truly prepared. You see, I'm all for studying our racial heritage. Most people are. But I'm also with Roy Wilkins, Thurgood Marshall and Bayard Rustin when they advise young Negro students to learn what the White students are learning *in addition,* or else they will be left out in the mad scramble for jobs. Justice Marshall declared that you're not going to compete in the world until you have training, just like everybody else, and hopefully better, because when you're a Negro, you've got to be better. Bayard Rustin even went so far as to question the advantages of the so-called soul courses in college, saying that in the real world they want to know about if you can do mathematics and write a correct sentence. I know that if I were an employer, I would hesitate to hire anyone who could not or would not do the work he was hired to do. Moreover, as more and more Negroes do qualify, the day will soon be past when we can blame our failures on our color. In other words, racial studies can certainly be advocated, but they should neither supersede nor supplant the regular studies, and they should be open to all who are interested. I wouldn't want anyone, Colored or White, to study music unless he feels he cannot resist it as I felt,

132

for the competition is intensely keen. One who adopts it as a profession should feel much like a potential minister when he gets his call to service. When the musical call comes, and the individual decides that he really does want to make music his ministry, I would suggest an exhaustive review of every aspect: harmony, harmonic analysis, form, counterpoint, fugue, musical history (including the history of Negro music), and so on.

Some years ago, one of my colleagues of the early jazz days came to me with a story of a Colored musician who had been engaged as an arranger because he was Colored and, therefore, was assumed to have an original slant on the music. He did very well at it for several years, despite his limited training. One day he happened to get into a discussion with someone who was quite able to talk about music in technical terms. He became quite enthusiastic during the conversation and exclaimed, "Say, this is great! I think I'll go and study harmony!" A little late in my opinion, but commendable, nonetheless.

One of my Negro friends who plays professionally in symphonic groups on the West Coast recently came to me with another problem. He had been trying to organize a Colored chamber music group, but had difficulty finding members willing to rehearse. Some wanted only to show up at the concert, sight-read the music, and collect the pay. Now this is something that not even the most famous and experienced artists dare to do; they all know the value of rehearsals. Jazz players often do it, of course, since improvisation has been one of their obligations, but in "serious" music one must stick to what is written, and the people who are so good they don't need to practice are rare indeed. In the end, my friend was forced to get an interracial group, which incidentally worked very well.

I am very pleased that I have become acquainted with the works of gifted younger composers like Hale Smith, Ulysses Kay, and others, but unfortunately for me and for the purposes of this discussion, I am not as yet familiar with the work being done by all of our young Negro composers. (So many composers never answer their mail!) Despite this, I have seen some scores and have heard some of their music, and much of this has been very encouraging, indeed! Several of the composers handle their material expertly from the viewpoint of craftsmanship and, creatively speaking, I think we can look forward to a bright future. In some instances, the

133

younger men remind me of myself when I was their age, experimenting, learning from everything possible, and trying to develop an individual form of expression.

Some of you possibly know that, for me, the so-called avant-garde is now the rear guard, for I studied with its high priest, Edgar Varese, in the 20's, and I was a devoted disciple. Some of my early compositions in that idiom were performed auspiciously in New York. I was amused recently when a writer heard one of my works and was upset because it was not in the avant-garde idiom. The writer said, "Time has passed Mr. Still by." Well, if this writer had done his homework, he would have known that it was I who recognized the handwriting on the wall many years ago, and voluntarily left the type of time he referred to, and I'm convinced I made the right decision.

I learned a great deal from the avant-garde idiom and from Mr. Varese but, just as with jazz, I did not bow to its complete domination. I had chosen a definite goal, namely, to elevate Negro musical idioms to a position of dignity and effectiveness in the fields of symphonic and operatic music. This would have been extremely difficult, or even impossible, had I chosen the avant-garde idiom. Through experimentation, I discovered that Negro music tends to lose its identity when subjected to the avant-garde style of treatment. I made this decision of my own free will, knowing very well that pressures would be brought to bear to make me follow the leader, and compose as others do. I have stuck to this decision, and I've not been sorry. American music is a composite of all the idioms of all the people comprising this nation, just as most Afro-Americans who are "officially" classed as Negroes are products of the mingling of several bloods. This makes us *individuals*, and that is how we should function, musically and otherwise. My personal feeling is that the avant-garde idiom as it stands is not the idiom of the future, no matter how its adherents try to convince me that I'm unsophisticated to think so. I've watched its deleterious effect on audiences and have noted that the general public, for whom music is supposed to be written, couldn't care less. I would urge young Afro-American composers to think of the avant-garde as a phase, not an end in itself, and if not a phase, a facet of composition.

Negroes have long been known as spontaneous creators. One has only to study the wealth of artistic innovations they have given to the world. Not every Negro is a spontaneous creator naturally, nor is everything all of us do superlative. We cannot lay claim to this distinction and neither can any other group of people, but we can evaluate the past, present and future in music, and begin again to write with heart instead of brains, with love instead of disdain, and with attention to spiritual as well as scientific values. Experimentation for the sake of experimentation can only produce a poor substitute for music, and we are now in need of *real* music, not contrived sounds. We need a new contemporary goal. I suggest that this goal be beauty, and I maintain that there is no substitute for inspiration. Every composer should work toward expressing his own personality in music. I shudder to think of the consequences if all of us were to start turning out music that is like the music of all the others. Such a trend has been observed in contemporary music. It is my hope that its end is near, and that sanity will reassert itself.

Afro-American composers, incidentally, have a wonderful opportunity to influence a trend toward sanity if they will make up their minds to return to the originality for which Negroes have become famous.

I cannot close without commenting on the current riotous conditions on our college campuses. In case you think they have nothing to do with Negro music, you are wrong. If they are allowed to continue without restrait, there will be no future for any of us, in music or anywhere else. When White students riot and display their ugliness on TV, the public immediately speaks of anarchy, of communism, and the hampering of the silent majority's right to gain an education. When Negroes riot, the same thoughts are present, plus other conclusions not amicable to us as a racial group. The unfortunate result of Negro rioting is that so often those who are the most ignorant, violent and unwholesome are constantly in the forefront of our TV screen. By whose wish: theirs or the TV medium? I cannot say. One thing is certain: their images create a climate of fear and distrust among their fellow Americans, White and Colored alike. Many White Americans know they are not typical, but there are some who are positive they *are* typical, and that they represent the Negro race. Without stopping to analyze the situation, they automatically cast all of us into the same mold. Of course, it affects Negro musicians and their music just as it adversely affects all decent Afro-Americans, in-

135

cluding the children yet unborn. In the end it will probably affect the rioters themselves. It has been said that the Negro students have been influenced by the White dissidents, but that it is the Negro students who will go to prison, while the Whites go free, and this is not an impossible theory, I think you will agree. To me, one of the most significant factors in this current trouble is that it came when there seemed to be no need for it. Negroes were already getting ahead as they qualified. The situation was not yet perfect, but it was improving, and it gave every indication of continuing to do so. There was enough of a climate of good fellowship first to make outsiders see some merit in the demands that were made by campus militants. Then, as the demands escalated and became more and more ridiculous, and as it became evident that people were coming from off-campus to incite trouble, even our friends began to lose patience. When it was noted that the ignorant were insisting upon dictating to the educated, and the inexperienced were demanding the right to direct the experienced, many formerly well disposed people were on the way to losing all their permissiveness. The picture was not an attractive one.

Only twice have I had encounters with the so-called Black militants, both times unpleasant ones. The first came during a general discussion of racial matters, when two young men found themselves in complete disagreement with me. Their displeasure came not in an orderly discussion, but in a rather belligerent verbal warfare. As I am now 74 years of age, and have been a Negro for all of the 74 years, I did not need people fifty years younger than I to tell me what it is, or what it should be, to be a Negro. The second encounter came when it was least suspected, in a college music class. I don't expect complete agreement with my views, though I do look for some respect. This I have received in every other student aggregation I have addressed, from elementary schools, even in deprived areas, to university audiences. Moreover, in this class there were only two belligerents. The rest were studious and appreciative. They did not seem to be in agreement with the militants on any count, although the militants seemed as if they were ready to do battle.

Those two should have known that they could do nothing to make me talk or compose differently, but perhaps they hoped to alter the good opinion of their classmates. Basically, they told me my music was not Negro music which, in their opinion, was the jungle-type sounds heard over a particular radio station in that city. All else was what they termed "Eur"-American music, rather than Afro-American. They also seemed disturbed because the clarinetists in the orchestras that played my music (one of them was the Royal Philharmonic of London) didn't play like Duke Ellington's clarinetist. Indeed, they seemed astonished that my compositions didn't sound like the Duke's! They were even a little sad when I told them they were not intended to sound that way. One of them prattled about the bourgeois and White man's music, while the other made it a point to let me know that he did not "identify" with my music, no doubt expecting me to be crushed by this verdict. He then made the separatist statement that we have grown up in America with only two different cultures, White and Black. This is a fallacious statement for, as you know, here in America, the melting pot, a large number of cultures may be found, gradually influencing each other. The Negro culture has definitely been influenced by Whites, just as White culture has been influenced by Negroes. In my opinion, we have both gained by the fusion, and who can define the exact line of demarcation?

The day after this second encounter, the Black Student Union asked for the resignation of their Negro instructor, despite the fact that students were then signing up for his next term course, and the enrollment had nearly doubled. The interesting angle was that the Black students themselves had requested the course with specifically a Negro instructor. The college had been fortunate enough to find a retired head of a music department from an eastern university, with a degree from the Oberlin Conservatory and almost forty years of teaching experience. The college and most of his students were pleased with his work. Only the two militants, they alone, wanted to drag his ideals down to their level, and thus limit the development of Negro music in general. This occurrence cast serious doubt on the sincerity, at least, of those militants. If they made a reasonable demand which was met by the college in good faith, shouldn't they have been properly receptive? Why should they, obviously the most unprepared in class, have assumed the task of dictating to their classmates? What actually were their motives? What were they trying to accomplish? Remembering that the two militants had almost succeeded in taking over the full discussion period, I wondered why they were so insistent on freedom of expression for themselves, while denying it to all the others.

They did not hesitate to insult others, but made it appear that a crime had been committed when their ideas were questioned. I confess that in one short class period, I lost whatever sympathy I might have had for militants.

Noting that this one little experience has multiplied and expanded to the level of violence on so many college campuses, I cannot blame the public in general for being so impatient with such hypocrisy. It is good to take pride in one's race, but is *this* pride? When these people begin to appreciate the good things that are available within America, to respect the rights of others, to develop a sense of true values and to talk about civil responsibility along with civil rights, then everyone will be willing to listen. Our forebears were willing to assume a share of the burden, along with the blessings. Why can't we? If it is clear that our attitude is changing in a constructive way, then perhaps the violent backlash which Billy Graham has predicted will never appear. At the very least, we might say that the idea of letting unprepared students choose their studies, choose their teachers, and even indicate what they want to be taught within a given subject is certainly open to question.

To all those who talk of separation, I would say again that I am now and forever against it. I am for integration. We're all Americans in our hearts, in our music, in our very being. At this point in our history we should begin to weigh, to analyze and to evaluate, all with a view to deciding whether or not we want to jump on bandwagons indiscriminately and to making up our minds as to what we actually do want. Of course many of us are frustrated! All of us are to some extent, and all of us probably will continue to be in some degree as long as we live. But, as Thurgood Marshall has so aptly remarked, we are not going to settle anything with guns, fire bombs or rocks. It appears now that many American Negroes feel that they are frustrated specifically because of White people and their attitude, so it seems to me that we should take a long look at White people in general to see whether this is entirely correct.

In my opinion, there are three broad categories into which White people will fit. The first type has not been given enough credit, and yet it is they who have done the most to help us up the ladder to full citizenship and success. They are the sympathetic ones who try just as hard as we do to make brotherhood a reality. I know

138

that I shall always be grateful to the many White friends who helped me. I could not have made it in a community solely of Negroes for the simple reason that Negroes did not have the facilities of the large orchestras, publishing houses and so on, which I needed in order to advance. White people made these facilities available to me in nearly every instance.

The second class of White persons is known to all of us as the uncompromising bigot. He is a difficult person to deal with, so he is best ignored.

He is still easier to take, however, than the third sort of person, the one who talks loudly about his commitment to brotherhood, enthusiastically welcomes you until you begin to measure arms with him. Then he surreptitiously opposes you while continuing to shout his love for his less fortunate brethren. He is the most frustrating, and least approachable of all. *Sneaky* would be the best word to describe him.

I've always found it wise to go my own way, doing the best that I can, and trusting that God will eventually show such people the errors of their ways, for I am convinced that we must all work together harmoniously. Only in this way can America's greatness reach its zenith. Make no mistake about it: the future of our music is tied immutably to that of the individual musician, and the future of the race as a whole is bound up in the future of America. What is good for our nation is good for the race. We must never let ourselves think otherwise, nor allow ourselves to be duped into a separatist philosophy, no matter how frustrated we may feel. We and our fellow Americans are in this together. As Americans with Negro blood, we are willing and able to contribute something of value to America. Those of us in the field of music know that our music has already proved to be a distinctive contribution. Our forebears contributed their sweat and their blood. Our sons have fought on foreign shores for the ideal of democracy. We have an investment in this nation. We own a share of it. Now is the time to decide: shall we protect that investment, or shall we destroy it?

W. G. S.

THE CATALOGUE OF WORKS

Date	Title	Approximate duration in minutes	Publisher

Works for the Stage

1927 LA GUIABLESSE (ballet) 30 ms.
Scenario by Ruth Page, after a Lafcadio Hearn tale based on a legend of the West Indian island of Martinique.
First performed on the Third Annual Festival of American Music in Rochester, New York, May 5, 1933: Dr. Howard Hanson, conductor; Thelma Biracree, solo dancer.
Requirements: 1 stage set; corps de ballet; 4 solo dancers; full orchestra.
Three of the dances from LA GUIABLESSE ("Dance of the Children", "Dance of Yzore and Adou" and "Entrance of Les Porteuses") comprise an orchestral suite which has often been played separately.

1930 SAHDJI (choral ballet) 45 CFI-ESM
Scenario by Alain Locke and Richard Bruce, on an African tribal subject.
First performed on May 22, 1931 in Rochester, New York: Dr. Hanson, conductor; Thelma Biracree, solo dancer.
Requirements: 1 stage set; corps de ballet: chorus; bass soloist; 3 solo dancers; full orchestra.

1934 BLUE STEEL (opera) 120 ms.
In three acts, this opera on a libretto by Carlton Moss and Bruce Forsythe was unperformed in its entirety (though short excerpts were presented on several concerts) and was later scrapped by the composer, who incorporated its musical material into other works.
Requirements: full orchestra, 3 stage settings, vocal soloists and chorus.

1937 LENOX AVENUE (ballet) 23 WGS Music
Scenario by Verna Arvey, descriptive of street scenes in New York's Harlem.
Originally commissioned by the CBS Network and first performed as a composition for radio over that Network on May 23, 1937. It was scored for reduced orchestra, narrator, chorus and piano soloist. The ballet version does not require a narrator, but does require 2 solo dancers and a corps de ballet. A piano-vocal score of this work was printed by J. Fischer & Bro., the original publishers, also an arrangement for small orchestra of the "Blues" episode. In addition, there are unpublished arrangements of the "Blues" for violin and piano, and for violin and orchestra.

1940   MISS SALLY'S PARTY (ballet)   30   ms.
Scenario by Verna Arvey, set in the Old South, and climaxed by a
Cakewalk.
First performed at the 11th Annual Festival of American Music
in Rochester, New York, on May 2, 1941: Dr. Hanson, conductor;
Thelma Biracree, solo dancer.
Requirements: 1 stage set, corps de ballet, full orchestra, 7 solo
dancers.

1941   TROUBLED ISLAND (opera in 3 acts)   120   ms.
Libretto by Langston Hughes, with additional text by Verna Arvey:
based on the life of Haiti's first Emperor, Jean Jacques Dessalines.
First performed at the New York City Center, Laszlo Halasz conducting, on March 31, 1949.
Requirements: 4 stage sets, chorus, full orchestra, 8 vocal soloists,
ballet.

1941   A BAYOU LEGEND (opera in 3 acts)   120   ms.
Libretto by Verna Arvey, inspired by an authentic legend of the
Biloxi region, concerning a man who fell in love with a spirit.
Requirements: 3 stage sets, full orchestra, chorus, 6 vocal soloists.

1943   A SOUTHERN INTERLUDE (opera in 2 acts)
                                             60   ms.
This short work, unperformed, has been scrapped by the composer
and its musical material incorporated into other works. The
libretto was by Verna Arvey, and its requirements were: 1 stage
set, reduced orchestra, small chorus, 4 vocal soloists.

1950   COSTASO (opera in 3 acts)   120   ms.
Libretto by Verna Arvey, set in Spanish-Colonial America and
inspired by a legend of that region.
Requirements: 4 stage sets, chorus, full orchestra, 10 vocal soloists,
ballet.

1951   MOTA (opera in 3 acts)   120   ms.
Libretto by Verna Arvey, a dramatization of intrigue within an
African tribe.
Requirements: 2 stage sets, full orchestra, chorus, 8 vocal soloists.

1956   THE PILLAR (opera in 3 acts)   120   ms.
Libretto by Verna Arvey on an American Indian theme.
Requirements: 3 stage sets, full orchestra, ballet, chorus, 10 vocal
soloists.

1958   MINETTE FONTAINE (opera in 3 acts)   120   ms.
Libretto by Verna Arvey, revealing the drama in the life of a
19th century prima donna of the old New Orleans Opera Company.
Requirements: 5 stage sets, full orchestra, chorus, 10 vocal soloists.

144

1962   HIGHWAY 1, U.S.A. (opera in 2 acts)   60   ms.
Libretto by Verna Arvey: an incident in the life of an American
family, set in a filling station near the highway.
First performed at the University of Miami under the direction of
Fabien Sevitzky on May 11, 1963.
Requirements: 1 stage set, chorus, reduced orchestra, 4 vocal
soloists.

1965   INCIDENTAL MUSIC for THE PRINCE AND THE MERMAID
                                                20   ms.
Composed for piano and consisting of four musical moods ("Song
of the Sea", "Waltz", "Minuet" and "Scherzo") this music was
adapted for a small instrumental combination and used at key
points during the course of Carol Stone's play, a fairy tale for
children.
It was first performed at San Fernando Valley (California) State
College in March, 1966.

Works for Orchestra

1921   THREE NEGRO SONGS   10   ms.
These songs, scored for reduced orchestra, were never performed
or published and have been discarded by the composer.
The titles of the songs were:
a. Negro Love Song
b. Death Song
c. Song of the Backwoods

1922   BLACK BOTTOM   10   ms.
Also discarded by the composer, this composition for chamber
orchestra was neither performed nor published.

1924   DARKER AMERICA   17   CFI-ESM
A symphonic poem for chamber orchestra, later scored for reduced
orchestra. It won a publication prize at the Eastman School of
Music and was first performed at an International Composers'
Guild concert at Aeolian Hall in New York City, Eugene Goossens
conducting, on November 28, 1926, after which the Musical
Courier, while acknowledging the fact that the composer was
still in his formative years, nonetheless added: "There is no doubt-
ing the man's power and his music on this particular occasion
was like a bright spot amid a lot of muddy grime."

1924   FROM THE LAND OF DREAMS   8   ms.
The three voices required for this dissonant composition did not
appear as solo voices, but instead were treated as orchestral instruments. Performed at an International Composers' Guild concert
in New York City on February 8, 1925 with Vladimir Shavitz
conducting, the music was praised by one critic who heard in it

145

a genuinely musical use of jazz motifs, and attacked by another writer who felt that Edgar Varese, Mr. Still's teacher, had driven out of him all the rollicking, entertaining and original music attributed to Negroes. The composer agreed with the latter verdict and scrapped the work.

Scored for woodwinds, strings, percussion, three female voices.

1925　FROM THE JOURNAL OF A WANDERER 20　　　　ms.
First performed at the North Shore Festival by Frederick Stock and the Chicago Symphony Orchestra in 1926, this five-movement suite has been discarded by the composer.

It was scored for full orchestra, and the titles of the individual movements were:
a. Phantom Trail
b. Magic Bells
c. Valley of Echoes
d. Mystic Moon
e. Devil's Hollow

1926　FROM THE BLACK BELT　　　　　　20　　　　　　CFI
The seven sections of this suite are:
a. Li'l Scamp
b. Honeysuckle
c. Dance
d. Mah Bones is Creakin'
e. Blue
f. Brown Girl
g. Clap Yo' Han's
On the occasion of its first performance by Georges Barrere's Little Symphony at the Henry Miller Theatre in New York City, March 20, 1927, Mr. Barrere warned the hearers that Mr. Still was a pupil of Edgar Varese, whereupon one critic wrote that there was nothing hyperprismic about the music, leading one to conclude that Mr. Still wrote it while his estimable mentor was occupied in listening to a League, a Guild, or perhaps a Philadelphia Orchestra concert and consequently had his back turned.

It was originally scored for small orchestra, but was later amplified and now is published for full orchestra.

1927　FROM THE HEART OF A BELIEVER　10　　　　ms.
One of the first of Mr. Still's musical affirmations of his belief in and devotion to, God. It was never performed or published, and has been scrapped by the composer.

1927　LOG CABIN BALLADS　　　　　　10　　　　　　ms.
In this suite, the three sections were titled:
a. Long To'ds Night
b. Beneaf de Willers
c. Miss Malindy

146

Georges Barrere conducted it with his Little Symphony at the Booth Theatre in New York City on March 25, 1928, when it was reviewed sympathetically. F. D. Perkins, in the New York Herald-Tribune, spoke of it as "conservative, distinctly tuneful and expressively effective, well orchestrated."

The composer, however, was dissatisfied and scrapped the piece. It was scored for three violins, viola, 'cello, bass, woodwinds, percussion.

1928   **AFRICA**   30   ms.

In three sections, "Land of Peace", "Land of Romance" and "Land of Superstition", this suite was an American Negro's attempt to present in music his concept of the land of his ancestors. It was first performed in 1930 by the Barrere Little Symphony in a reduced version, then scored for full orchestra and in that form performed at an American Composers' concert in Rochester, later in 1930. It was described by critics as being charming, characteristic and lyric. Also, it was noted that it marked an advance over the Still works heard previously.

It, too, was later discarded by the composer, despite the fact that it had been performed repeatedly, in whole or in part, since its creation.

It is for full orchestra.

1930   **AFRO-AMERICAN SYMPHONY**   28   Novello

In large measure due to the untiring efforts and faith of its first publisher, George Fischer, this symphony has become one of the best known of William Grant Still's compositions. Each of its four movements:

a. Moderato assai—Longing
b. Adagio—Sorrow
c. Animato—Humor
d. Lento, con risoluzione—Aspiration

is accompanied by a poem by Paul Laurence Dunbar, one of the composer's favorites. The third movement (animato) is the Scherzo so often played separately. The symphony was first performed by Howard Hanson on the American Composers' concert at the Eastman School of Music on October 29, 1931. It won instant favor from critics and public alike. Amy H. Croughton, in the Rochester Journal, wrote: "To give one such composer as Mr. Still an opportunity to have his composition heard and to hear them himself would justify the entire American Composers' movement."

It is scored for full orchestra. Conductor's score and parts were printed by J. Fischer & Bro., also a separate arrangement of the Scherzo for small orchestra. Novello, the present publisher, is bringing out a miniature study score.

147

1933   A DESERTED PLANTATION   15   Robbins

This suite for reduced orchestra in three sections:
a. Spiritual—based on "I Want Jesus to Walk With Me"
b. Young Missy
c. Dance
was introduced by Paul Whiteman and his orchestra at the Metropolitan Operahouse in New York City on December 15, 1933. It was accompanied by extracts from Paul Laurence Dunbar's "The Deserted Plantation" and was said to be "skillfully constructed music, in which the various possibilities in color and sonority obtainable from this type of orchestra are ably and effectively realized". (Francis D. Perkins in the New York Herald-Tribune.) A piano reduction of three excerpts only is published.

1933   EBON CHRONICLE   9   ms.

This orchestral poem was given a first performance by the Fort Worth (Texas) Symphony Orchestra under the direction of Paul Whiteman on November 3, 1936. The composer later discarded it. It was scored for full orchestra.

1935   THE BLACK MAN DANCES   10   ms.

Three movements make up this suite for orchestra. It was never performed or published and has now been discarded.

1936   DISMAL SWAMP   15 Theodore Presser Co.

A tone poem, descriptive of Virginia and North Carolina's great Dismal Swamp, forbidding at first glance, but possessing hidden beauty for those who penetrate its depths. Musically, this is expressed by "an atmospheric, ingenious development of a constantly repeated phrase", culminating in an impressive finale.
It is scored for full orchestra, and was first presented by Dr. Howard Hanson in Rochester on October 30, 1936.

1936   BEYOND TOMORROW   9   ms.

A melodic tone poem for orchestra, never performed or published.

1937   SYMPHONY IN G MINOR   25   WGS Music

Subtitled "Song of a New Race".
This, Mr. Still's second symphony, is a continuation of the earlier AFRO-AMERICAN SYMPHONY. Whereas the latter spoke of the American colored man of yesteryear, not far removed from slavery, the G MINOR SYMPHONY described the American colored people of today: a new race which is, in effect, a fusion of more than one racial element.
First performed by Leopold Stokowski and the Philadelphia Orchestra in Philadephia on December 10, 1937, it was reviewed as being "of absorbing interest, unmistakably racial in thematic material and rhythms, and triumphantly articulate in expressions of moods, ranging from the exuberance of jazz to brooding wist-

fulness" (Linton Martin in the Philadelphia Inquirer, December 11, 1937). In contrast, the Philadelphia Evening Bulletin for the same date found the third (Scherzo) movement lively and effective, but heard little suggestion of the rich and inventive idiom of the Negro race in it.

It is scored for full orchestra.

1940   CAN'TCHA LINE 'EM   10   ms.

This work, based on a folk theme, was commissioned by CBS and first performed over that radio network on February 17, 1940 on the program "American School of the Air".

It is scored for small orchestra.

1941   OLD CALIFORNIA   10   WGS Music

A capsule musical history of the state of California is given in this work: first, the Indian beginnings; second, the Spanish occupation with its gay dances and its religious devotion; third, the coming of the American—a time of strife proceeding to a period of peace and plenty for all.

It was composed at the request of Werner Janssen to honor the 160th birthday of the city of Los Angeles and was first performed by the Janssen Symphony Orchestra in Los Angeles on October 30, 1941, when it was enthusiastically received. It has been played many times since then, in the United States and abroad. The composer dedicated it to his dear friend and publisher, George Fischer.

It is scored for full orchestra.

1943   IN MEMORIAM: THE COLORED SOLDIERS WHO DIED FOR DEMOCRACY   6   MCA Music

This brief requiem for the colored soldiers proved to be one of the most successful of the more than a dozen works on patriotic themes commissioned by the League of Composers. From the time of its first performance by Arthur Rodzinski and the Philharmonic-Symphony of New York on January 5th and 7th, 1944, it has been played for many audiences in the United States and abroad, with generally favorable results. Olin Downes (in the New York Times for January 6, 1944) commented that the composer had written "with simplicity and feeling, without affectation or attitudinizing". Simon, in PM for the same date, wrote that "It says what it has to say directly and tellingly, and remains within the time limit without strain, as the other works in the series have not done."

It is scored for full orchestra.

1943   FANFARE FOR AMERICAN WAR HEROES
                                              1   ms.

For full orchestra, unperformed and unpublished.

149

1943 PAGES FROM NEGRO HISTORY   10   CFI
The three short sections in this suite ("Africa", "Slavery" and
"Emancipation") were composed for student orchestras, included
in the collection "Music of Our Time", and thus may be classed
as educational music. Performances have been frequent, but un-
reviewed.
It is scored for reduced orchestra.

1944 POEM FOR ORCHESTRA   15   MCA Music
Inspired by a concept of a world being re-born spiritually after
a period of darkness and desolation, the POEM FOR ORCHESTRA
was commissioned by the Fynette H. Kulas American Composers'
Fund for the Cleveland Symphony Orchestra and first performed
by that organization under the direction of Rudolph Ringwall on
December 7th and 9th, 1944. It was described as building to "a
musical climax of hope and coming to spiritual consciousness in a
singing melody of strings" (Cleveland Plain-Dealer, January 1,
1945) and as having "lovely, lyrical passages and stirring, forthright vitality" (Musical America, January 10, 1945).
It is scored for full orchestra.

1944 BELLS   7   MCA Music
Originally published by Delkas for piano solo, this composition
was arranged by the composer for reduced orchestra. Its two sections are "Phantom Chapel" and "Fairy Knoll", and it was first
performed in its entirety by the St. Louis Symphony Orchestra
under Vladimir Golschmann, on November 29th and 30th, 1946.
At that time Harry Burke, writing in the St. Louis Globe-Democrat
(November 30, 1946) commented: "What is not a commonplace
in concerts is great music by a Negro composer . . . So simple,
so sincere, so colorful. So dramatic in its texture of tone!"

1944 FESTIVE OVERTURE   10   WGS Music
From among thirty - nine especially composed scores submitted
anonymously for the Cincinnati Symphony Orchestra's Jubilee
Season competition, three d istinguished judges (Eugene Goossens,
Pierre Monteux and Deems Taylor) were unanimous in their
choice of William Grant Still's FESTIVE OVERTURE as the winner of the prize. First performed on January 19th and 20th, 1945
by Eugene Goossens (to whose memory the Overture is now dedicated) and the Cincinnati Symphony, the critics gave their approval
to the music, mentioning its "American flavor" and its "irre-
pressible march rhythm". (The Cincinnati Post and Cincinnati
Enquirer for January 20, 1945.) The work has defied the oblivion
sometimes accorded to contest winners, and has been played many
times.
It is scored for full orchestra.

1945 SYMPHONY No. 5   25   WGS Music

At the time it was composed, this was Dr. Still's Third Symphony. He later decided to discard it and substitute a completely new Third Symphony. In the course of time, and after the creation of Symphony No. 4, he decided to revise it as Symphony No. 5, in which form it still exists.

The work, scored for full orchestra, is subtitled "Western Hemisphere". Its four movements depict 1. The vigorous, life-sustaining forces of the Hemisphere (brisky) 2. The natural beauties of the Hemisphere (slower, and with utmost grace) 3. The nervous energy of the Hemisphere (energetically) 4. The overshadowing spirit of kindness and justice in the Hemisphere (moderately). This composition was first performed by the Oberlin College Orchestra under the direction of Robert Baustian, at the celebration of the composer's 75th birthday on campus, a delayed event which took place on November 9, 1970.

1945 FANFARE FOR THE 99th FIGHTER SQUADRON

                                          1   ms.

Scored for wind instruments, this short musical tribute was played by Leopold Stokowski and the Los Angeles Philharmonic Orchestra in the Hollywood Bowl on July 22, 1945.

1946 ARCHAIC RITUAL   20   WGS Music

Thematically unified, as was the earlier AFRO-AMERICAN SYMPHONY, the ARCHAIC RITUAL emphasizes the transformation and interweaving of motifs, so that each movement of the Suite (1. "Chant" 2. "Dance Before the Altar" 3. "Possession") is irrevocably tied to the others. Morover, each movement builds, so that the opening Chant gives way to a spirited dance rhythm which, in turn, proceeds to a more frenzied section in which the worshippers are possessed by spirits.

This was first played by Izler Solomon and the Los Angeles Philharmonic Orchestra in the Hollywood Bowl on August 25, 1949 and is scored for full orchestra.

1947 SYMPHONY No. 4 (AUTOCHTHONOUS) 27   WGS Music

As the subtitle indicates, the Fourth Symphony has its roots in our own soil, but rather than being aboriginal or indigenous, it is intended to represent the spirit of the American people. The composer has described its four movements in this way: 1. Moderately: The spirit of optimism and energy 2. Slowly: pensive, later animated in a folky way 3. With a graceful lilt: humorous 4. Slowly and reverently: love of mankind.

This work is dedicated to one of the composer's early teachers, Maurice Kessler of Oberlin.

First performed by Victor Alessandro and the Oklahoma City Symphony Orchestra on March 18, 1951.

Scored for full orchestra.

1947 WOOD NOTES   20   SMC
Poems by the Southern poet, J. Mitchell Pilcher, inspired each of
the four sections of this suite: 1. "Singing River" 2. "Autumn
Night" 3. "Moon Dusk" 4. "Whipporwill's Shoes". It was dedi-
cated to another of the composer's early teachers at Oberlin, F. J.
Lehmann.
First performed by Arthur Rodzinski and the Chicago Symphony
Orchestra on April 22nd and 23rd, 1948 when the Chicago Daily
News described it as "pleasant music, with an occasional flash of
personality". It was performed in a version for full orchestra,
but later published for small orchestra.

1948 DANZAS DE PANAMA   15   SMC
Unique in the literature for string quartet, this suite makes use of
percussive effects, when the players beat on their instruments to
simulate the sound of native drums. The four sections (a. "Tamborito" b. "Mejorana y Socavon" c. "Punto" d. "Cumbia y
Congo") are all based on authentic Panamian dance themes (some
of Negro origin) collected by Elisabeth Waldo, whose string
quartet first performed them at the Los Angeles County Museum
on May 21, 1948.
The suite is published for string orchestra as well as for string
quartet.

1957 THE AMERICAN SCENE   50   WGS Music
Five descriptive suites for young Americans, scored for full orchestra, and titled as follows:
        Suite 1:   The East
                   a. On the Village Green
                   b. Berkshire Night
                   c. Manhattan Skyline
        Suite 2:   The South
                   a. Florida Night
                   b. Levee Land
                   c. A New Orleans Street
        Suite 3:   The Old West
                   a. Song of the Plainsmen
                   b. Sioux Love Song
                   c. Tribal Dance
        Suite 4:   The Far West
                   a. The Plaza
                   b. Sundown Land
                   c. Navaho Country
        Suite 5:   A Mountain, a Memorial and a Song
                   a. Grand Teton
                   b. Tomb of the Unknown Soldier
                   c. Song of the Rivermen
These suites have not yet been performed in their entirety. How-

152

ever, excerpts from most of them have been broadcast or played in concert by orchestras and (in some cases) by concert bands. The excerpts which the composer has arranged for band are: "Tomb of the Unknown Soldier", "A New Orleans Street", "Berkshire Night", "Tribal Dance" and "Grand Teton".

1957 **LITTLE RED SCHOOLHOUSE**   15   SMC
Adapted from a previous work, "Pages from a Mother's Diary", LITTLE RED SCHOOLHOUSE now consists of five sections: 1. "Little Conqueror" 2. "Egyptian Princess" 3. "Captain Kidd Jr." 4. "Colleen Bawn" 5. "Petey". Each section was intended to describe one of the students at a little red schoolhouse, so important a part of America's history. It was performed first at Redlands University in California, under the direction of Edward Tritt, on March 30, 1957. One reviewer spoke of the music as being "marked by imaginative, energetic and impish qualities usually associated with the innocence, imagery and high spirits of childhood."
It is scored for full orchestra, and is published for orchestra and in a band arrangement also.

1957 **SERENADE**   8   WGS Music
Commissioned by the Great Falls (Montana) High School and originally scored for a high school orchestra, this work was later adapted for full orchestra, and also arranged for flute, strings and piano. It was first played in the original version at Great Falls High School on May 7, 1958 and later performed repeatedly in the two subsequent versions.

1958 **SYMPHONY No. 3**   25   WGS Music
This symphony was composed to fill the gap when the composer discarded his first Symphony No. 3, which later was revised and became the Symphony No. 5. This new third symphony is subtitled "The Sunday Symphony", and consists of four movements as follows:
    1. Moderately: The awakening
    2. Very slowly: Prayer
    3. Gaily: Relaxation
    4. Resolutely: Day's end—and a new beginning.
It is scored for full orchestra and is as yet unperformed and unpublished.

1960 **PATTERNS**   15   WGS Music
The over-all title of this suite for chamber orchestra refers to the rather persistent rhythmic designs in its five sections, each of which was developed from the germ of a particular rhythmic theme. The individual titles of the movements are: a. "Magic Crystal" b. "A Lone Teardrop" c. "Rain Pearls" d. "Tranquil Cove" e. "Moon-gold".
The suite was first played by Ernst Gebert and the Inglewood

(California) Symphony Orchestra on April 23, 1961, and was reviewed as being a work "of imaginative character and pervasive beauty".

1960   THE PEACEFUL LAND   9   American Music
                                                     Edition

Critics spoke of this tone poem as being "quiet, expressive, undramatic, genuine and nonshowy" when it was given its first performance by Fabien Sevitzky and the University of Miami Symphony Orchestra on October 22nd and 23rd, 1961.
It was the winner of a prize offered jointly by the National Federation of Music Clubs and the Aeolian Music Foundation for a symphonic composition dedicated to the United Nations.
It is scored for full orchestra.

1962   LOS ALNADOS DE ESPANA   12   WGS Music
Spanish-Colonial life in the Western Hemisphere was the inspiration for this orchestral suite, as yet unperformed and unpublished. The colonies were known as "Stepchildren of Spain", and yet their life was colorful and of a quality not to be found again. The suite, comprising four selections: (a. "Prologo y narracion" b. "El Valle Escondido" c. "Serenata" d. "Danza") in a sense pays tribute to the composer's maternal grandfather, a Spaniard with holdings in Florida.
It is scored for full orchestra.

1962   PRELUDES   12   WGS Music
Scored for string orchestra, flute and piano, this suite is also in the form of a solo for piano. The tempo indications on each of its five sections are: 1. Moderately fast 2. Moderately slow 3. Delicately 4. Moderately 5. Energetically.
The PRELUDES were first performed by George Berres and the Westchester String Symphony in Los Angeles on May 26, 1968.

1965   THRENODY: IN MEMORY OF JAN SIBELIUS
                                        4   WGS Music
Requested by Fabien Sevitzky and first performed by him and the University of Miami Symphony Orchestra on March 14th and 15th, 1965, this short requiem won immediate approval from audiences and critics. In 1966 it was broadcast over the Finnish National Radio.
It is scored for full orchestra.

1965   MINIATURE OVERTURE   2   WGS Music
This was one of five short overtures written by five different American composers to celebrate the inaugural concert of the Greater Miami Philharmonic Orchestra, Fabien Sevitzky conducting, on October 17th and 18th, 1965.
It is scored for full orchestra.

1970 CHOREOGRAPHIC PRELUDE   5   WGS Music
Scored for string orchestra, flute and piano, this ingratiating
work was introduced by the composer and ensemble at a Los
Angeles County Museum concert on January 25, 1970. It emphasizes a percussive type of rhythm, so characteristic of primitive
dance ceremonials.

Works for Orchestra with Soloists or Chorus

1925 LEVEE LAND   10   ms.
The first performance of this three movement work, with text by
the composer and Florence Mills as vocal soloist, took place at an
International Composers' Guild concert in New York's Aeolian
Hall, Eugene Goossens conducting, on January 24, 1926. It was
one of the very first efforts to elevate the elements of jazz to
symphonic form, and it attracted a large audience of notables.
The New York World commented: "Curious and elemental were
these songs by this brilliant young Negro composer, plaintive in
part, blue, crooning and sparkling with humor, and Miss Mills
gave them a perfect interpretation."
This was scored for soprano solo, two violins, woodwinds, tenor
banjo, piano and percussion.
(N. B. This composition is not to be confused with the LEVEE
LAND which was composed many years later, as a part of THE
AMERICAN SCENE.)

1935 KAINTUCK'   13   WGS Music
Commissioned by the League of Composers and dedicated to Verna
Arvey, KAINTUCK' (though composed for piano solo and full
orchestra) received its initial performance on two pianos at a
Los Angeles Pro Musica concert on October 28, 1935, when
critics recognized it as "ingratiating music", "imbued with a languorous atmosphere properly typical of the Old South". Several
auspicious orchestral performances followed in different parts of
the country.

1938 SONG OF A CITY
Albert Stillman is the author of the words to the chorus which
concludes this rousing symphonic work, published separately for
solo voice and piano and for chorus and piano under the titles of
RISING TIDE and VICTORY TIDE (SSATBB, SATB AND
TTBB) by J. Fischer & Bro., now handled by Belwin.
The composition in its entirety, unperformed in its present form,
is an adaptation for full orchestra of the Theme Music for the
New York World's Fair 1939, written on commission and played
in the Perisphere for the duration of the Fair.

1940 **AND THEY LYNCHED HIM ON A TREE 19**   WGS Music
In this massive work, the full orchestra is joined by a Negro
chorus, a white chorus, narrator and contralto soloist to plead,
as Leopold Stokowski once said, for tolerance and the brotherhood
of man. The text is by Katherine Garrison Chapin. First performed by Artur Rodzinski at Lewisohn Stadium in New York
and enthusiastically received by audience and critics, the music
was considered by Robert Simon to be "the most ambitious effort
yet heard from its skillful composer". Added Howard Taubman,
"Mr. Still has written with utter simplicity and with deep feeling."

1941 **PLAIN-CHANT FOR AMERICA**   10   WGS Music
When he was asked to compose a work for the Centennial of the
New York Philharmonic Orchestra, Mr. Still decided to make a
setting of another poem by Katherine Garrison Chapin, for baritone,
full orchestra and organ. In that form, it was performed first by
Sir John Barbirolli and the New York Philharmonic on October
23rd and 24th, 1941. It received an unquestionable ovation and
critical approval. More than a quarter of a century later, the
composer substituted a chorus for the baritone soloist, and in
this new form it was given its initial hearing by Werner Torka-
nowsky, the New Orleans Philharmonic-Symphony Orchestra and
Dillard University Chorus on April 16, 1968. It was then described
as being just as timely as when first conceived, and its patriotic
theme even more appealing to listeners than at its inception.

1942 **THOSE WHO WAIT**   10   ms.
For chorus and full orchestra, on a text by Verna Arvey, and as
yet unperformed and unpublished. This work is a musical conversation, question and answer style, dealing with racial concepts
and solutions.

1946 **WAILING WOMAN**   10   ms.
For full orchestra, chorus and soprano soloist, on a text by Verna
Arvey, and as yet unperformed and unpublished.
An expression of the common cause of Jewish and colored people,
and of the sympathy which brings them together.

1948 **FROM A LOST CONTINENT**   15   WGS Music
Dr. Still's long interest in the legend of the lost continent of Mu,
said to have been engulfed in the Pacific Ocean thousands of years
ago, led him to attempt an imaginative concept of what its music
may have been. To give an archaic feeling and to avoid incongru-
ity, he used special syllables instead of an English text. The four
sections in this work are: 1. "Song of Worship" 2. "Song for
Dancers" 3. "Song of Yearning" 4. "Song of Magic".
This composition, scored for reduced orchestra, was first performed

156

in its entirety with *piano* and chorus on May 22, 1953, by the Choral Guild of San Jose (California) under the direction of LeRoy V. Brant. The first performance with orchestra was given over the I. N. R. (Flemish division) in Brussels, Belgium on March 27, 1955.

1954 THE LITTLE SONG THAT WANTED TO BE A SYMPHONY
                                              19   WGS Music
The Little Song, only four notes long, gives up its early dream of becoming a symphony in order to become a part of the lives of the children of America, and to bring them together in brotherhood. Basically a series of variations in the styles characteristic of each child's heritage (i.e., American Indian, Bayou dwellers, Oriental, Latin-American, Afro-American, Italian-American, big city youth, mountain folk) this composition is scored for narrator, three female voices and reduced orchestra, with extra parts available so that it may also be used with a full orchestra. The text is by Verna Arvey.
The work has won the approval of children and adults in many performances, the first by Theodore Russell and the Jackson (Mississippi) Symphony Orchestra on February 15, 1955.

1954 A PSALM FOR THE LIVING   10   Bourne Co.
For chorus and orchestra, on a text by Verna Arvey, based on the premise that God is not remote, but lives among us, guiding and inspiring our lives and achievements. It requires a reduced orchestra, but is often performed with piano accompaniment, as printed for S. A. T. B. The orchestral material is on rental.

1955 RHAPSODY   15   ms.
As yet unperformed and unpublished, this composition for soprano soloist and full orchestra was commissioned by the Southwide Conference for Mattiwilda Dobbs. It is on a text by Verna Arvey, detailing the advance of a woman from girlhood to maturity, with a growing awareness of brotherhood as the ultimate aim of mankind.
Its four sections are: 1. "Pastorale" 2. "Romance" 3. "Lullaby" 4. "Paean".
The work is dedicated to the memory of the composer's beloved son-in-law, Larry Allyn Headlee.

1956 ENNANGA   15   WGS Music
For harp solo and full orchestra, or string orchestra and piano. The word "Ennanga" is the name of an African harp. This is a suite in three movements, inspired by African music but not drawing literally on it for thematic material. It was first performed by Lois Adele Craft, to whom it is dedicated, in Los Angeles on October 12, 1958. It was reviewed as being "pleasantly melodic and, in feeling, related to Negro Spirituals. The content has drive and manages to sound convincing."

157

1962 **THE PATH OF GLORY** 15 ms.
For bass-baritone soloist and full orchestra, and on a text by
Verna Arvey, this work deals with the glory and fall of the
Aztec Empire. It consists of a Prologue and four sections: "In-
vocation", "Call to Battle", "Judgement" and "Elegy", separated
by Interludes.
The composition is as yet unperformed and unpublished.

1967 **CHRISTMAS IN THE WESTERN WORLD (LAS PASCUAS)**
20 SMC
For voices, string orchestra or string quartet and piano, or simply
for voices and piano. Nine of the songs in this compilation are
adapted from authentic Christmas folk tunes from various countries in the Western Hemisphere, while the tenth, the climactic one,
is an original William Grant Still song with text by Verna Arvey.
Titles of the individual sections are: "A Maiden was Adoring
God, the Lord"; "Ven, Niño Divino"; "Aguinaldo"; "Jesous
Ahatonhia" (oldest known Christmas carol on the North American
continent); "Tell Me, Shepherdess"; "De Virgin Mary Had a
Baby Boy"; "Los Reyes Magos"; "La Piñata"; "Glad Christmas
Bells"; "Sing, Shout, Tell the Story!"

Works for Band

1945 **FROM THE DELTA** 8 MCA Music
A short suite for band consisting of three sections: "Work Song"
(also arranged for orchestra by the composer); "Spiritual" and
"Dance".
Richard Franko Goldman and the Goldman Band first performed
this work at a Central Park Mall concert in New York City on
June 17, 1947.

1951 **TO YOU, AMERICA!** 11 SMC
Commissioned by the United States Military Academy for the
Sesquicentennial Celebration at West Point, this symphonic band
work was first played by the USMA Band, the composer conducting,
on February 17, 1952. That same year it won for its composer a
Freedoms Foundation Award.
The composer dedicated it to Col. Francis E. Resta and the USMA
Band. "Musically speaking", he wrote, "it is a development of a
single theme, energetic at the beginning and progressing to a
majestic, chorale-like Finale, pointing to a glorious national
destiny."

1963 **FOLK SUITE FOR BAND** 8 Bourne Co.
The Negro Spirituals on which this work is based are: "Get On
Board, Little Children", "Deep River", "The Old Ark's a Mover-
in' ", and "Sinner, Please don't Let This Harvest Pass".
It is scored for symphonic band and was first performed by Dale

158

Eymann and the Los Angeles Bureau of Music Symphonic Band in Los Angeles on August 18, 1963.

1967   LITTLE RED SCHOOLHOUSE   15   SMC
An arrangement by the composer for symphonic band of the earlier orchestral suite, described previously.

Chamber Music

1943   SUITE FOR VIOLIN AND PIANO   15   MCA Music
Each of the three movements in this composition was inspired by the work of a Negro artist. "African Dancer" (the first movement) by Richard Barthe's dancing figure; "Mother and Child" by Sargent Johnson's touching portrait; and "Gamin", by Augusta Savage's mischievous boy. It was first performed by Louis Kaufman, to whom it is dedicated, in Boston on March 15, 1944 and in New York's Town Hall on March 18, 1944, when it was said that "the music assumed the character of the subjects and was an adroit and interesting contribution to modern compositions."
An orchestral version of this work is available on rental.

1945   INCANTATION AND DANCE   5   CFI
First performed by Lloyd Rathbun, to whom it is dedicated, this atmospheric work for oboe and piano has been widely played since its publication.

1946   PASTORELA   11   Witmark
Again, for violin and piano, this composition was intended to give a musical picture of a California landscape, sometimes languorous, sometimes whimsical. It too was first performed by Louis Kaufman in Town Hall, New York, March 14, 1947, and it too is available on rental in an orchestral version.

1948   DANZAS DE PANAMA   15   SMC
This work is published for string orchestra. The individual dances (based on folk themes collected by Elisabeth Waldo) are: Tamborito, Mejorana, Punto, Cumbia y Congo.

1948   MINIATURES   12   Oxford U. Press
For flute, oboe, piano: based on folk tunes of the Western Hemisphere and dedicated to Sir John and Lady Barbirolli.
a. I Ride an Old Paint (U.S.A.)
b. Adolorido (Mexico)
c. Jesus Is a Rock In a Weary Land (U.S.A.)
d. Yaravi (Peru)
e. Frog Went a 'Courtin' (U.S.A.)

1954   ROMANCE   3   Bourne Co.
A melodic piece for saxophone and piano.

1957 FOUR INDIGENOUS PORTRAITS   10   ms.
For string quartet and flute.
a. North American Negro (an original theme in the style of a Spiritual)
b. South American Negro (based on Brazilian Negro themes)
c. South American Indian (based on Peruvian and Brazilian themes)
d. North American Indian (an original theme in the style of American Indian folk music).

1960 LYRIC STRING QUARTET   9   ms.
1. Moderately 2. Moderately slow (based on an Inca melody) 3. Moderately fast.
This quartet is dedicated to the composer's friend, Joachim Chassman.

1962 VIGNETTES   11:30   SMC
For oboe, bassoon and piano. Composed for Lady Evelyn Barbirolli.
a. Winnebago Moccasin Game (U.S.A.: Wisconsin)
b. Carmela (U.S.A.: early California)
c. Peruvian Melody (South America)
d. Clinch Mountain (U.S.A.: Southern Mountain Region)
e. Garde Piti Mulet La—also known as M'sieu Banjo (U.S.A.: Louisiana)

1962 FOLK SUITE #1   8:52   SMC
For flute, piano and string quartet.
1. Bambalele (Brazil)
2. Sometimes I Feel Like a Motherless Child (U.S.A.)
3. Two Hebraic Songs.

1962 FOLK SUITE #2   9   SMC
For flute, clarinet, 'cello and piano.
1. El Zapatero (U.S.A.: early California)
2. Mo'le (Peru)
3. Mom'zelle Zizi (U.S.A.: Louisiana)
4. Peruvian Melody (Inca)

1962 FOLK SUITE #3   5:04   SMC
For flute, oboe, bassoon and piano.
1. An Inca Dance (Peru)
2. An Inca Song (Peru)
3. Bow and Arrow Dance Song (U.S.A., Santo Domingo Pueblo, N.M.)

1962 FOLK SUITE #4   5:30   ms.
For flute, clarinet, 'cello and piano.
1. El Monigote (Venezuela)
2. Anda Buscando de Rosa en Rosa (Mexico)
3. Tayeras (Brazil)

1968   LITTLE FOLK SUITE from the WESTERN HEMISPHERE
                              2:30   SMC
       For brass quintet.
       1. Where Shall I Be When the Great Trumpet Sounds? (U.S.A.)
       2. En Roulant Ma Boule (French Canadian)

1968   LITTLE FOLK SUITE from the WESTERN HEMISPHERE
                              3:45   SMC
       #1, for string quartet.
       a. Salangadou (U.S.A., Creole)
       b. El Capotin (U.S.A., early California)

1968   LITTLE FOLK SUITE from the WESTERN HEMISPHERE
       #2, for string quartet.
       a. El Nido (Argentina)
       b. Sweet Betsy from Pike (U.S.A.)

1968   LITTLE FOLK SUITE from the WESTERN HEMISPHERE
       #3, for string quartet.
       a. Aurore Pradere and Tant Sirop est Doux (U.S.A. and Mar-
          tinique)
       b. Wade in the Water (U.S.A.)

1968   LITTLE FOLK SUITE from the WESTERN HEMISPHERE
       #4, for string quartet.
       a. Los Indios and Yaravi (Brazil; Peru)
       b. The Crawdad Song (U.S.A.)

1968   LITTLE FOLK SUITE from the WESTERN HEMISPHERE
       #5, for string quartet.
       a. Tutu Maramba (Brazil)
       b. La Varsoviana (U.S.A.: Spanish Colonial)

                        Works for Piano

1936   THREE VISIONS   11   WGS Music
       a. Dark Horsemen
       b. Summerland
       c. Radiant Pinnacle
       "Summerland" has been arranged for small and for full orchestra,
       also for flute, violin, viola, 'cello and harp.
       There is also an arrangement of "Summerland" for organ, made
       by Edouard Nies-Berger.

1938   QUIT DAT FOOL'NISH   2   Belwin
       A short encore piece.

1939   SEVEN TRACERIES   17   WGS Music
       a. Cloud Cradles
       b. Mystic Pool

161

c. Muted Laughter
d. Out of the Silence
e. Woven Silver
f. Wailing Dawn
g. A Bit of Wit
"Out of the Silence" has been arranged for flute, piano and string orchestra by the composer.
"Muted Laughter" is now included in Bernice Frost's book, "Piano Repertoire", a collection of piano classics from the XVIth to the XXth century, published by J. Fischer & Bro.

1939 SWANEE RIVER   2   Robbins
Included in a book called "29 Modern Piano Interpretations of 'Swanee River' ".

1944 BELLS   6   MCA Music
a. Phantom Chapel
b. Fairy Knoll
There is also an orchestral version of this work.

1946 MARIONETTE   1   MCA Music
This is included in the book, "U.S.A. 1946".

1951 FIVE ANIMAL SKETCHES
Included in the book, "Music for Early Childhood".

1964 RING PLAY   1   Belwin
A teaching piece, included in Bernice Frost's book, "Twentieth Century Piano Music".

Works for Organ

1962 REVERIE   3 F. Rayner Brown
1963 ELEGY   3 F. Rayner Brown

Works for Accordion

1960 ARIA   5 Sam Fox Pub. Co.
      LILT   4 Pietro Deiro Pub.

Works for Voice or Voices and Piano

1928 WINTER'S APPROACH   3   G. Schirmer
For solo voice and piano, on a poem by Paul Laurence Dunbar.

1928 BREATH OF A ROSE   5   G. Schirmer
For solo voice and piano, on a poem by Langston Hughes.

1937 TWELVE NEGRO SPIRITUALS   25   Handy Bros.
For solo voice and piano, on traditional themes.
a. I Got a Home in-a Dat Rock b. All God's Chillun Goe Shoes

c. Camp Meetin' d. Didn't My Lord Deliver Daniel? e. Good
News f. Great Day g. Gwinter Sing All Along the Way h. Keep
Me From Sinkin' Down i. Listen to the Lams j. Lord, I Want to
Be a Christian, k. My Lord Says He Is Goin' to Rain Down Fiah
l. Peter, Go Ring Dem Dells.
These Spiritual arrangements were re-published in their entirety
for solo voice and piano by Francis Day & Hunter, in London.
Three of them (Gwinter Sing All Along the Way, Keep Me From
Sinkin' Down and Lord, I Want to Be a Christian) were arranged
by the composer for S. A. T. B. and published in that form by
Handy Bros.

1939   RISING TIDE (also known as VICTORY TIDE)—see the listing
under "Song of a City" in the section on orchestral works with
added vocalists.

1941   HERE'S ONE   4   John Church Co.
For solo voice and piano, a setting of a Negro Spiritual; words
traditional.
This was also arranged by the composer and published for
S. A. T. B.

1941   CARIBBEAN MELODIES   60   Oliver Ditson Co.
For solo voices, chorus, piano and percussion instruments. Texts
from the folk of several West Indian islands, as collected by Zora
Neale Hurston.
The concluding song, "Carry Him Along" was published separately
for S. A. T. B.

1944   BAYOU HOME   3   Robbins
For solo voice and piano, text by Verna Arvey.

1946   THE VOICE OF THE LORD   5   Witmark
For tenor soloist, mixed chorus and piano.
A setting of Psalm 29, composed for the Park Avenue Synagogue
in New York City and first performed there by Cantor David J.
Putterman and choir on May 10, 1946. Included in An Anthology
"Synagogue Music by Contemporary Composers", G. Schirmer.

1938   EV'RY TIME I FEEL THE SPIRIT   2   Galaxy
For solo voice and piano, an arrangement of a traditional Negro
Spiritual.

1948   MISSISSIPPI   3   ms.
For voices and piano, on a text by Verna Arvey.
Performed on the "Sound Off" program over the ABC radio net-
work (the U.S. Army broadcast) on July 26, 1948.

1949   SONGS OF SEPARATION   12   WGS Music
For solo voice and piano, based on texts by five Negro poets.
a. Idolatry (Arna Bontemps)

163

b. Poeme (Philippe-Thoby Marcelin of Haiti)
c. Parted (Paul Laurence Dunbar)
d. If You Should Go (Countee Cullen)
e. A Black Pierrot (Langston Hughes)
"Art songs rich with the freedoms of beautiful melody, dramatic force and lyric intensity—" Marilyn Tucker in the San Francisco Chronicle, May 18, 1970.
There is a version of this vocal suite for reduced orchestra and soloist, on rental. The composer has made an additional arrangement for solo voice, string quartet and piano.

1950 LAMENT   3   Silver Burdett
For women's trio and piano, on a text by Verna Arvey.
Included in the book, "American Music Horizons".

1950 UP THERE   1½   Silver Burdett
For solo voice and piano, on a text by Verna Arvey.
Included in the book, "World Music Horizons".

1950 SINNER, PLEASE DON'T LET THIS HARVEST PASS
For S. A. T. B. and piano. Included in "Let Music Ring", edited by Peter W. Dykema, published by California State Department of Education, Sacramento, 1950.

1952 SONG FOR THE VALIANT   3   WGS Music
For solo voice and piano, text by Verna Arvey.

1953 SONG FOR THE LONELY   4   ms.
For solo voice and piano, text by Verna Arvey.

1953 GRIEF   3   Oliver Ditson Co.
For solo voice and piano, text by LeRoy V. Brant.

1956 CITADEL   2   ms.
For solo voice and piano, poem by Virginia Brasier Perlee.

1956 I FEEL LIKE MY TIME AINT LONG   3   Theodore Presser
For S. A. T. B. and piano, an arrangement of a traditional Nego Spiritual.

1956 IS THERE ANYBODY HERE?   3   Theodore Presser
For S. A. T. B. and piano, an arrangement of a traditional Negro Spiritual.

1961 THREE RHYTHMIC SPIRITUALS   9   Bourne Co.
Published separately for S. A. T. B. Also available, a version for solo voice and orchestra.
a. Lord, I Looked Down the Road
b. Hard trials
c. Holy Spirit, Don't You Leave Me.

1961 FROM THE HEARTS OF WOMEN   9   ms.
A suite for solo voice and piano, on a text by Verna Arvey.
There is also a version for solo voice, flute, oboe, string quartet
and piano.
a. Little Mother (A child sings to her doll).
b. Midtide (A woman reaches middle age).
c. Coquette (A young girl flirts).
d. Bereft (A mother loses her son).

1965 ALL THAT I AM   2   ms.
A hymn for S. A. T. B. and piano on a text by Verna Arvey.

1968 SONG OF THE HUNTER   1   Holt, Rinehart &
                                            Winston
For solo voice and piano; included in the textbook, "Exploring
Music".

1968 GOD'S GOIN' TO SET THIS WORLD ON FIRE
                                       1   Holt, Rinehart &
                                            Winston
For solo voice and piano; included in the textbook, "Exploring
Music". It is an arrangement of a traditional Negro Spiritual.

1968 YOUR WORLD   3   Ginn & Co.
For voices and piano, a setting of a poem by Georgia Douglas
Johnson, included in the textbook, "The Magic of Music".

1971 MY BROTHER AMERICAN   2 American Book Co.
This song, set to words by Verna Arvey, is included in the 7th
grade music textbook, in the series called New Dimensions in
Music.

1971 WE SANG OUR SONGS (The Fisk Jubilee Singers 1871-1971)
                                       3   ms.
This work was commissioned for the Centennial Celebration at
Fisk University on October 6, 1971. It is set to a text by Verna
Arvey.

Note

* *Full* orchestra, with some few exceptions, means:
  strings
  3 flutes, interchangeable with piccolo
  2 oboes
  English Horn
  2 clarinets
  bass clarinet
  2 bassoons
  4 horns
  3 trumpets

3 trombones
tuba
timpani
percussion
harp
celeste

V.A.

---

* *Reduced* orchestra, generally speaking, means that the wood-winds and brasses are in pairs.

Publishers

American Music Edition — 263 East 7th Street, New York, New York 10009
Belwin, Inc — Rockville Center, L.I., New York 11571
Bourne Company — 136 West 52nd Street, New York, New York 10019
CFI (Carl Fischer, Inc.) — 56-62 Cooper Square, New York, New York   They also
    distribute for the Eastman School of Music: ESM
C. C. Birchard Company — 285 Columbus Avenue, Boston 16, Mass.
F. Rayner Brown — 2423 Panorama Terrace, Los Angeles, California 90039
Francis, Day & Hunter — 138-140 Charing Cross Road, London, W.C. 2, England
G. Schirmer, Inc. — 609 - 5th Avenue, New York, New York 10017
Galaxy — 50 West 24th Street, New York, New York 10010
Ginn & Company — Boston, Mass. 02117
Handy Brothers Music Company — 1650 Broadway, New York, New York 10019
Holt, Rinehart & Winston — 383 Madison Avenue, New York, New York 10017
MCA Music — 225 Park Ave., So., New York, New York 10003
Novello & Company, LTD — 27 Soho Square, London, W.1, England
    American representative: Belwin, Inc.
Oxford University Press — 44 Conduit Street, London, W.1, England
Pietro Deiro — 133 - 7th Avenue South, New York, New York 10014
Robbins Music Corporation — 799 Seventh Avenue, New York, New York 10019
Sam Fox Publishing Company — 11 West 60th Street, New York, New York 10023
Silver Burdett — Morristown, New Jersey 07960
SMC (Southern Music Publishing Company, Inc.) 1619 Broadway, New York,
    New York 10019
Theodore Presser, Oliver Ditson and John Church Companies — Bryn Mawr, Pa.
WGS Music (William Grant Still Music) — 1262 Victoria Avenue, Los Angeles,
    California 90019
Witmark (Music Publishers Holding Corporation — RCA Building, Rockefeller
    Center, New York, New York 10020

V.A.

THE DISCOGRAPHY

William Grant Still . . . Discography

1940-1941   Scherzo from the AFRO-AMERICAN SYMPHON, recorded by Howard Hanson and the Eastman-Rochester Symphony Orchestra for Victor Records, no. 2059-B.

1940-1941   Excerpts from the SEVEN TRACERIES, recorded by Verna Arvey, pianist, for Co-Art Records, no. 5037 A and B.

1942   The Flirtation from LENOX AVENUE, ployed by the Hancock Ensemble under the direction of Loren Powell and issued by the Hancock Foundation at USC, no. 395.

Early Forties   The Blues from LENOX AVENUE, recorded by Artie Shaw and his orchestra for Victor Records, no. 27411 A and B.

1944   Scherzo from the AFRO-AMERICAN SYMPHONY, recorded by Leopold Stokowski and the All-American Orchestra for Columbia Records, no. 11992-D.

1948   HERES' ONE and the Blues from LENOX AVENUE, recorded by Louis Kaufman (violinist) and Annette Kaufman (pianist) in an American album for Vox, no. 667-A.
In 1950, Concert Hall Records re-issued this album as an L.P., under the title "Contemporary American Violin Music", no. H-1640, CHS 1140.

1948   Work Song from FROM THE DELTA, recorded by Morton Gould and his symphonic band for Columbia Records, no. 4519-M, CO 39622.

1952   The AFRO-AMERICAN SYMPHONY, recorded by Karl Krueger and the Vienna Opera Orchestra for New Records, Inc. NRLP 105
and
Excerpts from the SEVEN TRACERIES, LENOX AVENUE and THREE VISIONS, played by Gordon Manley, Pianist.

1952   TO YOU, AMERICA! recorded by Lt. Col. Francis E. Resta and the West Point Symphonic Band and included in the recordings of the Pittsburgh International Contemporary Music Festival, issued by ASCAP for non-commercial use by educational institutions.

Date unavailable   HERE'S ONE, recorded by Robert McFerrin, baritone, for Riverside records, no. 812.

1959   A tape of the FOURTH SYMPHONY (AUTOCHTHONOUS) available from the National Association of Educational Broadcasters, to educators only. Taken from a 1959 UNESCO concert in Denver, the composer conducting.

1960	Suite from the ballet SAHDJI, recorded by Howard Hanson with the Eastman Rochester Orchestra and the Eastman School Chorus for Mercury Records, no. MG 50257 B.

1960 Suite from the ballet SAHDJI, recorded by Howard Hanson with the Eastman Rochester Orchestra and the Eastman School Chorus for Mercury Records, no. MG 50257 B.

1963 HERE'S ONE, recorded by Bill Mann (tenor) and Paul Mickelson (organist) for Word Records, Inc. W-3061 LP.

1965 The AFRO-AMERICAN SYMPHONY, recorded by Karl Krueger and the Royal Philharmonic Orchestra of London, for the Society of the Preservation of the American Musical Heritage, no. MIA-118.

1970 FESTIVE OVERTURE, recorded by Arthur Bennett Lipkin and the Royal Philharmonic Orchestra of London for Composers' Recordings, Inc., CRI SD 259.

1970 SONGS OF SEPARATION, recorded by Cynthia Bedford (mezzo soprano) and the Oakland Youth Symphony Orchestra under the direction of Robert Hughes for Desto Records, no. DC-7107.

1970 THREE VISIONS, played by Natalie Hinderas, pianist, on a Desto record, no. DC-7102.

1971 SUITE FOR VIOLIN, PASTORELA, SUMMERLAND, BLUES (from "Lenox Avenue"). Folk Music from North America (CARMELA and HERE'S ONE) played by Louis and Annette Kaufman on an Orion Stereo record (ORS 7152) Box 243321, Los Angeles, California, 90024.

1971 DARKER AMERICA recorded by Siegfried Landau and the Music from Westchester Symphony Orchestra for Turnabout Records.

1971 Excerpts from Suite #3 from "THE AMERICAN SCENE" (THE OLD WEST, including SONG OF THE PLAINSMEN, SIOUX LOVE SONG, and TRIBAL DANCE), recorded by the All-state group of the National Music Camp at Interlochen.

1972 ENNANGA recorded by Lois Adele Craft (harpist), pianist Annette Kaufman, and string quartet; SONGS OF SEPARATION and SONG FOR THE LONELY recorded by Claudine Carlson accompanied by Georgia Akst; DANZAS DE PANAMA recorded by Louis Kaufman, George Berres, Alex Neiman and Terry King for Orion Stereo Records (ORS 7278).

V.A.

THE BIBLIOGRAPHY

A. GENERAL BIBLIOGRAPHY

Apel, Willi. *The Harvard Dictionary of Music*. Cambridge, Massachusetts: The Harvard University Press, 1944.

Arvey, Verna. *William Grant Still: Studies of Contemporary American Composers*. New York: J. Fischer & Bro., 1939. Includes an Introduction by John Tasker Toward.

Arvey, Verna. *Choreographic Music: Music for the Dance*. New Work: E. P. Dutton & Co., Inc., 1941.

ASCAP Biographical Dictionary. New York: 1948, 1952, 1966.

Austin, William W. *Music in the Twentieth Century*. New York: W. W. Norton & Co., 1966.

Bagar, Robert and Louis Biancolli. *The Concert Companion*. New York: McGraw-Hill Book Company, Inc., 1947.

Baker's Biographical Dictionary of Musicians. New York: G. Schirmer, 1940.

Baldwin, Lillian. *A Listener's Anthology of Music Vol. II*. New York: Silver Burdett Company, 1948.

Bardolph, Richard. *The Negro Vanguard*. New York: Rinehart & Company, Inc., 1959.

Barlow, Harold and Sam Morgenstern. *A Dictionary of Musical Themes*. New York: Crown Publishers, 1948.

Bauer, Marion. *Twentieth Century Music*. New York: G. P. Putnam's Sons, 1933.

Beaumont, Cyril W. *Complete Book of Ballets*. New York: G. P. Putnam's Sons, 1938.

Bergman, Peter M. and Mort N. *The Chronological History of the Negro in America*. New York: A Mentor book, published by the New American Library, 1969.

Block, Maxine. *Current Biography*. New York: The H. W. Wilson Company, 1941.

Blom, Eric. *Grove's Dictionary of Music and Musicians Vol. VIII*. New York: St. Martin's Press, Inc. 1962.

Blume, Frederick. *Die Musik in Geschichte und Gegenwart, Vol. II*. Kassel: Barenreiter-Verlag, 1949.

Boyden, David D. *The History and Literature of Music: 1750 to the Present*. Berkeley, California: University Extension Press, 1959.

Brawley, Benjamin. *The Negro Genius*. New York: Dodd, Mead and Company, 1937.

Bull, Storm. *Index to Biographies of Contemporary Composers*. New York: The Scarecrow Press, Inc., 1964.

Butcher, Margaret Just. *The Negro in American Culture*. New York: Alfred A. Knopf, 1956.

Carpenter, Paul S. *Music, An Art and a Business*. Norman, Oklahoma: University of Oklahoma Press, 1949.

Chase, Gilbert. *America's Music from the Pilgrims to the Present*. New York: McGraw-Hill Book Company, Inc., 1955.

Colee, Nema Weathersby. *Mississippi Music and Musicians*. Magnolia, Mississippi: Sponsored by the Mississippi Federation of Music Clubs, 1949.

Collaer, Paul. *A History of Modern Music*. Cleveland, Ohio: The World Publishing Company, 1955.

Cowell, Henry. *American Composers on American Music*. Palo Alto, California: Stanford University Press, 1933.

Cuney Hare, Maud. *Negro Musicians and Their Music*. Washington, D. C.: The Associated Publishers, Inc., 1936.

Deakin, Irving. *Ballet Profile*. New York: Dodge Publishing Company, 1936.

de Lerma, Dominique-Rene. *Black Music in Our Culture*. Ohio: Kent State University Press, 1970.

Dizionario Ricordi della musica e dei musicisti. Milano, Italia: Ricordi, 1959.

Embree, Edwin R. *American Negroes, A Handbook*. New York: The John Day Company, 1942.

Embree, Edwin R. *Thirteen Against the Odds*. New York: The Viking Press, 1944.

172

Engle, Donald L. *Collier's Encyclopedia Vol. XVIII*. New York: P. F. Collier and Son, 1955.

Ewen David. *American Composers Today*. New York: H. W. Wilson Company, 1949.

Ewen, David. *The Complete Book of 20th Century Music*, Revised edition. Englewood Cliffs, New Jersey: Prentice-Hall, Inc., 1959.

Ewen, David. *Composers of Today*. New York: The H. W. Wilson Company, 1934.

Ferguson, Blanche E. *Countee Cullen and the Negro Renaissance*. New York: Dodd, Mead and Company, 1966.

Franklin, John Hope. *From Slavery to Freedom*. New York: Vintage Books (Random House) 1969.

Goss, Madeleine. *Modern Music Makers*. New York: E. P. Dutton & Co., Inc., 1952.

Grabbe, Paul. *The Story of Orchestral Music and Its Times*. New York: Grosset & Dunlap, 1942.

Guzman, Jessie Parkhurst. *1952 Negro Yearbook*. New York: William H. Wise & Company, Inc., for Tuskegee Institute.

Handy, W. C. *Father of the Blues*. New York: The Macmillan Company, 1941.

Hansen, Peter S. *An Introduction to Twentieth Century Music*. Boston: Allyn and Bason, Inc., 1961.

Howard, John Tasker. *Our Contemporary Composers*. New York: Thomas Y. Crowell Company, 1942.

Howard, John Tasker and James Lyons. *This Modern Music*. New York: Thomas Y. Crowell Company, 1942.

Hughes, Langston and Milton Meltzer. *Black Magic, a Pictorial History of the Negro in American Entertainment*. Englewood Cliffs, New Jersey: Prentice-Hall, 1967.

Hughes, Langston. *Famous Negro Music Makers*. New York: Dodd, Mead and Company, 1955.

Jacobs, Arthur. *A New Dictionary of Music*. Chicago: Aldine Publishing Company, 1962.

Kaufmann, Helen L. *From Jehovah to Jazz: Music in America from Psalmody to the Present Day*. New York: Dodd, Mead and Company, 1937.

Kaufmann, Helen L. *The Story of One Hundred Great Composers*. New York: Grosset and Dunlap, 1943.

Kaufmann, Schima. *Everybody's Music*. New York: Thomas Y. Crowell Company. 1938.

Locke, Alain. *The Negro and His Music*. Bronze booklet no. 2. Washington, D. C.: The Associates in Negro Folk Education, 1936.

Landis, Beth and Lara Hoggard. *Exploring Music, the Junior book*. New York: Holt, Rinehart & Winston, 1968.

Larson. Clotye M. *Marriage Across the Color Line*. Chicago: Johnson Publishing Company and New York: Lancer Books. Copyright 1945 and 1965.

Machlis, Joseph. *Introduction to Contemporary Music*. New York: W. W. Norton and Company, 1961.

Marrocco, W. Thomas and Arthur C. Edwards. *Music in the United States*. Dubuque, Iowa: William C. Brown, publisher, 1968.

McKinney, Howard D. *Music and Man*. *New York:* American Book Company, 1956.

Miller, Hugh M. *History of Music* (in the College Outline series) New York: Barnes & Noble, Inc., 1947, 1953.

Mize, J. T. H. *Who is Who in Music?* Chicago, 1951.

Mueller, John T. H. *The American Symphony Orchestra, a Social History of Musical Taste*. Indiana University Press, 1951.

Noble, Peter. *The Negro in Films*. London: British Yearbooks Ltd. 30, Cornhill, E. C. 3.

Oderigo, Nestor R. Ortiz. *Panorama de la Music Afroamericana*. Buenos Aires: Editorial Claridad 1944.

Oderigo, Nestor R. Ortiz. *Rostros de Bronce*. Argentina: Compania General Fabril Editora, 1965.

Osgood, Henry O. *So This is Jazz*. Boston: Little, Brown and Company, 1926.

173

Parry, Hubert H. *The Evolution of the Art of Music.* New York: D Appleton and Company, 1923.

Posell, Elsa Z. *American Composers.* Boston: Houghton Mifflin Company, 1963.

Quarles, Benjamin. *The Negro in the Making of America.* New York: Collier Books (The Macmillan Company) 1964.

Read, Gardner. *Thesaurus of Orchestral Devices.* London: Sir Isaac Pitman & Sons, Ltd. 1953.

Reis, Claire. *American Composers, a Catalogue.* New York: The United States section of the International Society for Contemporary Music, 1932.

Reis, Claire. *Composers in America.* New York: The Macmillan Company, 1938, revised 1947.

Reis, Claire R. *Composers, Conductors and Critics.* New York: Oxford University Press, 1955.

Richardson, Ben. *Great American Negroes.* New York: Thomas Y. Crowell Company, 1945.

Rosenfeld, Paul. *An Hour With American Music.* Philadelphia: J. B. Lippincott Company, 1929.

Ross, David J., Jr. *Great Negroes Past and Present. Chicago:* Afro-Am Publishing Company, Inc., 1963.

Rossi, Nick and Robert Choate. *Music of Our Time.* Boston: Crescendo Publishing Company, 1969.

Rugg, Harold. *An Introduction to Problems of American Culture.* Boston: Ginn and Company, 1931.

Sandved, Kjell Bloch. *The World of Music.* London: The Waverly Book Co., Ltd., 1965. Norwegian version: *Musikkens Verden.* Oslo: 1951. Also published by Abradale Press in New York in extended form, as a four-volume illustrated Encyclopedia.

Salazar, Adolpho. *Music in Our Time.* New York: W. W. Norton Company, 1946.

Sargeant, Winthrop. *Jazz Hot and Hybrid.* New York: Arrow Editions, 1938.

Scholes, Percy A. *The Oxford Companion to Music.* London: Oxford University Press, 1938.

Schuller, Gunther. *Early Jazz: Its Roots and Musical Development.* New York: Oxford University Press, 1968.

Southern, Eileen. *The Music of Black Americans: a History.* New York: W. W. Norton and Company, Inc., 1971.

Southern, Eileen. *Readings in Black American Music.* New York: W. W. Norton and Company, Inc., 1971.

Spaeth, Sigmund. *A Guide to Great Orchestral Music.* New York: The Modern Library (Random House) 1943.

Spaeth, Sigmund. *A History of Popular Music in America.* New York: Random House Press, 1948.

Stearns, Marshall. *The Story of Jazz.* New York: The Oxford University Press, 1956.

Thompson, Oscar. *The International Cyclopedia of Music and Musicians.* New York: Dodd, Mead and Company, 1952.

Ulrich, Homer and Paul A. Pisk. *A History of Music and Musical Style.* New York: Harcourt, Brace and World, Inc., 1963.

Waters, Ethel. *His Eye Is On the Sparrow.* New York Doubleday, 1951.

Watson, Jack M. and Corinne. *A Concise Dictionary of Music.* New York: Dodd, Mead and Company, 1965.

Watters, Lorrain and Louis G. Wersen, William C. Hartshorn, L. Eileen McMillan, Alice Gallup, Frederick Beckman. *The Magic of Music,* Book 6. Boston, Massachusetts: Ginn and Company, 1968.

Wodson, Carter G. and Charles H. Wesley. *The Story of the Negro Retold.* Washington, D. C. Associated Publishers, 1935.

Who's Who in America. All editions since 1942. Chicago: The A. M. Marquis Company.

P.H.S.

Unpublished Material

Simpson, Ralph Ricardo. *William Grant Still—The Man and His Music.* Ph. D. dissertation, Michigan State University, 1964.

Slattery, Paul Harold. *A Comparative Study of the First and Fourth Symphonies of William Grant Still.* Masters Thesis, San Jose College, 1969.

Thompson, Leon Everette. *The Music of William Grant Still.* Ph. D. dissertation, University of Southern California, 1966.

P.H.S.

Books Consulted for Definitions Only

Cook, Deryck. *The Language of Music.* London: Oxford Press, 1959.

Dallin, Leon. *Techniques of Twentieth Century Composition.* Dubuque, Iowa: William C. Brown Company, 1957.

Forte, Allen. *Contemporary Tone Structures.* New York: Bureau of Publications, Teachers College, Columbia University, 1955.

Jones, George Thaddeus. *Music Composition.* Evanston, Illinois: Summy-Birchard Company, 1963.

Meyer, Leonard B. *Emotion and Meaning in Music.* Chicago: The University of Chicago Press, 1956.

Ratner, Leonard G. *Music: The Listener's Art.* San Francisco: McGraw-Hill Book Company, 1966.

Sessions, Roger. *The Musical Experience of Composer, Performer, Listener.* New York: Atheneum Press, 1965.

P.H.S.

B. By William Grant Still

AN AFRO-AMERICAN COMPOSER'S POINT OF VIEW, in the book, *American Composers on American Music,* edited by Henry Cowell, 1933.

THE ART OF MUSICAL CREATION, in The Mystic Light (Rosicrucian Magazine) July, 1936.

THE AMERICAN COMPOSER, in the Baton, March, 1937.

ARE NEGRO COMPOSERS HANDICAPPED? The Baton, November 1937.

FOR FINER NEGRO MUSIC, Opportunity, May, 1939.

A NEGRO SYMPHONY ORCHESTRA. Opportunity, September 1939.

A RECORDED CONVERSATION in the Co-Art Turntable (Beverly Hills) August 1942.

THE NEGRO AND HIS MUSIC, in the War Worker, (Los Angeles) October 1943. This was the text of a speech delivered at UCLA on a seminar dealing with Music and the War. It was also printed in the book, Writers' Congress, published by the University of California and the Hollywood Writers' Mobilization.

THE MEN BEHIND AMERICAN MUSIC, the Crisis, January 1944.

HOW DO WE STAND IN HOLLWOOD? Opportunity, Spring issue, 1945.

POLITICS IN MUSIC, in Opera, Concert and Symphony, August 1947.

AMERICAN MUSIC AND THE WELL-TIMED SNEER, Opera, Concert and Symphony, May 1948.

A SYMPHONY OF DARK VOICES, Opera, Concert and Symphony, May, 1947.

CAN MUSIC MAKE A CAREER? Negro Digest, December 1948.

MUSIC, A VITAL FACTOR IN AMERICA'S RACIAL PROBLEMS, in the Australian Musical News for November 1, 1948. This was reprinted in the Oberlin Alumni Magazine for March, 1950.

THE COMPOSER NEEDS DETERMINATION AND FAITH, Etude, January 1949.

THE STRUCTURE OF MUSIC, Etude, March, 1950.

LA MUSICA DE MI RAZA . . . Musica, Bogota, Columbia, Vol. 1.

FIFTY YEARS OF PROGRESS IN MUSIC, Pittsburgh Courier, November 11,
    1950. This was reprinted in Denmark, as NEGRENE i AMERIKANSK
    MUSIK, in the Dansk Musiktidsskrift, Copenhagen 1951.
TOWARD A BROADER AMERICAN CULTURE, a convention address to the
    American Symphony Orchestra League. Printed in the American Symphony
    Orchestra League Newsletter Vol. 6 no. 1, then reprinted in the Southwestern
    Composers' Journal 1955-56, Vol. 1, no. 2.
THE HISTORY AND FUTURE OF BLACK AMERICAN MUSIC STUDIES:
    PRACTICES AND POTENTIALS . . . condensed from the speech delivered
    at Indiana University's Seminar on Black Music, June 21, 1969 . . . printed
    in the Music Bulletin of Lincoln University, Pa. for August 4, 1969, Vol. 11
    no. 4.
THE NEGRO MUSICIAN IN AMERICA, in the Music Educators' Journal . . .
    January, 1970.
A COMPOSER'S VIEWPOINT:
    de Lerma, Dominique-Rene. Chapter by William Grant Still in *Black Music
    in Our Culture*. Ohio: Kent State University Press, 1970.

V.A.

C. By William Grant Still
(in collaboration with Verna Arvey)

NEGRO MUSIC IN THE AMERICAS . . . Revue Internationale de Musique . . .
    Bruxelles, May - June 1938.
DOES INTERRACIAL MARRIAGE SUCCEED? The Negro Digest, April 1945.
THE KING IS DEAD—LONG LIVE THE KING! New York Stadium Concerts
    Review, June 25, 1945.
SERIOUS MUSIC: NEW FIELD FOR THE NEGRO, in Variety, January 1, 1955.
MODERN COMPOSERS HAVE LOST THEIR AUDIENCE: WHY? in the Austra-
    lian Musical News for July, 1956. This was reprinted in the Music Journal
    1966 Annual under the title of THE LOST AUDIENCE FOR NEW MUSIC.
OUR AMERICAN MUSICAL RESOURCES in Showcase (Music Clubs Magazine)
    Fall, 1961 issue.
MY ARKANSAS BOYHOOD,in the Arkansas Historical Quarterly, Autumn, 1967.
ANSWER TO A QUESTIONNAIRE, in Arts and Society: published by University
    Extension: University of Wisconsin, 1968. Issue dedicated to the Arts in the
    Black Revolution.

V.A.

D. About William Grant Still

THE BALLETS OF WILLIAM GRANT STILL, by Verna Arvey, in the Fall 1937
    issue of The New Challenge, a Literary Quarterly. This was later included in
    the book, CHOREOGRAPHIC MUSIC, by Verna Arvey, published by Dutton
    in 1941.
WILLIAM GRANT STILL (photographs) in Flash! November 15, 1938.
IS THERE A PLACE FOR NEGROES IN CLASSICAL MUSIC? by Verna Arvey
    in Upbeat, January 1939.
WILLIAM GRANT STILL: CREATIVE ASPECTS OF HIS WORK, by Verna
    Arvey in the January-March 1938 issue of the Dillard University Arts Quarterly.
STUDIES IN CONTEMPORARY AMERICAN MUSIC: WILLIAM GRANT STILL,
    by Verna Arvey, published by J. Fischer & Bro., New York, 1939.
WILLIAM GRANT STILL, CREATOR OF INDIGENOUS AMERICAN MUSIC,
    by Verna Arvey in the Chesterian (London) May-June 1939.
WILLIAM GRANT STILL, AMERICAN COMPOSER, by Verna Arvey, in the
    Co-Art Turntable (Beverly Hills) February, 1942.

176

MEET THE COMPOSER: WILLIAM GRANT STILL, by Isabel Morse Jones in Musical America for December 25, 1944. This was reprinted in the Negro Digest for May, 1945 under the title of FROM TIN PAN ALLEY TO OPERA.

VISITS TO THE HOMES OF FAMOUS COMPOSERS, No. 3: WILLIAM GRANT STILL, by J. Douglas Cook in Opera, Concert and Symphony for November 1946.

STILL OPERA POINTS THE WAY, by Verna Arvey, in Music Forum and Digest for August, 1949.

PHYLON PROFILE XXIII: WILLIAM GRANT STILL, COMPOSER, by Miriam Matthews, in Phylon, published by Atlanta University, second quarter, 1951.

NATIVE OF LITTLE ROCK IS WIDELY CELEBRATED NEGRO COMPOSER, by Clara B. Kennan in the Arkansas Gazette, August 5, 1951.

COMPOSER PROVES THERE'S NO COLOR LINE IN MUSIC WORLD, by John Fleming in the Arkansas Gazette, August 9, 1953.

CLASSIFIED CHRONOLOGICAL CATALOGUE OF WORKS BY THE UNITED STATES COMPOSER, WILLIAM GRANT STILL, in the Boletin Interamericano de Musica, November 1959, published by the Pan American Union in Washington, D. C. This was later reprinted in Volume 5 of Compositores de America, also published by the Pan American Union.

WITH HIS ROOTS IN THE SOIL, by Verna Arvey, in the International Musician for July 1963.

HARMONY AIM OF NEGRO COMPOSER, by Art Seidenbaum in the Los Angeles Times, September 7, 1963.

BRIDGING A MUSICAL GAP, by Patterson Greene in the Los Angeles Herald-Examiner for September 8, 1963.

WILLIAM GRANT STILL, by Joyce Lippey and Walden E. Muns in the Music Journal, November, 1963.

38 YEARS OF SERIOUS MUSIC, by Louie Robinson in Ebony Magazine, February 1964.

AN OUTSTANDING ARKANSAS COMPOSER, WILLIAM GRANT STILL, by Mary D. Hudgins in the Arkansas Historical Quarterly, Winter 1965.

WILLIAM GRANT STILL: 50 YEARS OF MUSIC, by Boris Nelson in the Toledo (Ohio) Blade, May 2, 1965.

MUSICAL PREMIERE DUE AT E. L. A., by Jerry Doernberg in the San Gabriel Valley edition of the Los Angeles Times, May 13, 1965.

WILLIAM GRANT STILL, THE DEAN OF NEGRO COMPOSERS, by Mary D. Hudgins in the Arkansas Gazette, January 30, 1966.

STILL HAS LIVED THROUGH MUSICAL CHANGES, by Karen Monson in the Los Angeles Herald-Examiner, January 24, 1970.

STILL IS GRATEFUL FOR TIN PAN ALLEY DAYS, by Henry Butler in the Indianapolis News, March 6, 1970.

A chapter in the book, MUSIC OF OUR TIME, by Nick Rossi and Robert A. Choate, published by Crescendo Publishing Company, Boston, 1969.

COMPOSERS SINCE 1900, by David Ewen, published by H. W. Wilson Company, 1969.

V.A.

A FESTIVAL FOR THE FUTURE

PROGRAMMING THE WORKS OF
WILLIAM GRANT STILL

Symphonic conductors have often complained, "There isn't enough material available from Negro composers." Neither quantitatively nor qualitatively is this actually the case. Why such materials remain largely unknown and therefore unpresented is an issue for musical sociologists to untangle.

The purpose of this volume is to set the matter straight, at least for William Grant Still.

The purpose of this section is to assist programmers in the future by suggesting a number of feasible programs for sampling the work of William Grant Still.

Each program has been planned around the unifying thread of Still's multicultural approach. Each program has been planned in terms of the effective placement and length of the works involved. Each program has been planned with a view to economy of personnel in performance. All the works listed are ready for performance.

This plan was worked out as a proposal for a Festival of the Works of William Grant Still to commemorate Still's seventy-fifth birthday. It was undertaken at the suggestion of the musical director of the Voice of America, who has for over thirty years championed the performances of American composers (and incidentally of Still's work) on a national and even international basis.

Who will be first to make the Festival a reality, and thereby to demonstrate Still's great overarching vision of the "Fusion of Musical Cultures in America?"

R. B. H.

179

NOTES: PROGRAM I

A varied program, full of contrasts.

The frequently played *Festive Overture* has been characterized by Eugene Goossens as "Elgarian"; actually it is, as Still says, "pure American". A curtain raiser.

Well known and well recorded, the *Afro-American Symphony* is firmly based on Negro idioms, with the blues a principle theme. Each of the movements expresses a definite and different mood.

Poem for Orchestra, one of Still's key works, is in a highly personal idiom. The harmonizations and thematic materials are easy to listen to; the development is musically interesting, full of departures in form. After a sombre beginning, the work moves to describe a bright and illuminated place as man turns from desolation to God.

Essentially a theme and variations. *The Little Song that Wanted to be a Symphony* is built on a story about a song born in music-land which came to earth and wanted to become a symphony. The variations are in the styles of different peoples—Indian, Creole, Japanese, and so on.

The *Symphony #4* does not confine itself to Negro themes. Still calls them "indigenous themes" or themes from the soil. The music takes on a cathedral like quality. The ending is big but lifting.

An American program, except for the *Poem,* which is intended to touch on universals.

PROGRAM I

Orchestral Works

Duration

(1944) *Festive Overture* 10

(1930) *Afro-American Symphony* 28

(1944) *Poem for Orchestra* 15

(1954) *The Little Song that Wanted
to be a Symphony* 19

(1947) *Symphony #4* 27

NOTES: PROGRAM II

An economical dance program which can utilize the same dancers for all three ballets.

Sahdji is Still's response to his first hearing of authentic African songs. At the time Alain Locke brought him the scenario, Still could only find three books on African music in the New York Public Library. The ballet is in two parts. Substantial and very theatrical. When placed first on the program, the members of the chorus can go home after the first work is concluded.

La Guiablesse, a small-scale work, required Still to devise and create music which would suggest its Martinique setting. You won't find the folk themes in the West Indies—they are all Still. Requires a trap door for performance.

Miss Sally's Party is a "funny" ballet, danced in "everyday" southern costumes. Its music is closely allied to the popular music of the Nineteenth Century.

A full program.

PROGRAM II

An Evening of Ballets and Stage Works

(1930) *SAHDJI*

Choral Ballet, scenario by Alain Locke and Richard Bruce on an African tribal subject.

    1 stage set, corps de ballet, chorus, bass soloist, 3 solo dancers, full orchestra, 45 minutes.

(1927) *LA GUIABLESSE*

Scenario by Ruth Page after a Lafcadio Hearn tale based on a legend of the West Indian Island of Martinque.

    1 stage set, corps de ballet, 4 solo dancers, full orchestra, 30 minutes.

(1940) *MISS SALLY'S PARTY*

Ballet, scenario by Verna Arvey, set in the Old South and climaxed by a Cakewalk.

    1 stage set, corps de ballet, full orchestra, 7 solo dancers, 30 minutes.

NOTES: PROGRAM III

All works on this program do not require a full orchestra but can be performed by reduced orchestra and various smaller combinations.

Preludes has consistently "entertained" audiences. It begins in a modernistic idiom and becomes more consonant as it moves forward.

Darker America shows Still emerging from the influences of Varese and reaching toward a personal idiom. In this work he found it was difficult to use the Negroid idiom in conjunction with a modern idiom—it loses its identity.

From the Black Belt, a melodic work made up from some short tunes and some longer ones about the very old South.

Out of the Silence, one of the *7 Traceries,* is a meditative, quiet, atmospheric piece in Still's most personal idiom. It grows out of his interest in occultism.

Wood Notes, a consonant suite, very Southern, speaks of some Alabama scenes. Inspired by a collaboration with the white Southern poet, J. Mitchell Pilcher.

Serenade is a romantic work, begun as a cello work for Gregor Piatagorsky, but metamorphosed into an orchestral work with an attractive melody for the cello section.

Choreographic Prelude, a longtime idea of Still's, works out a percussive theme. There are no lyrical passages, only an exciting and rhythmic dythram and striking finale.

PROGRAM III

Works for Reduced Orchestra

		Duration
(1962)	*Preludes*	12
(1924)	*Darker America*	17
(1926)	*From the Black Belt*	20

(1939)	*Out of the Silence*	6
(1947)	*Wood Notes*	20
(1959)	*Serenade*	8
(1970)	*Choreographic Prelude*	5

NOTES: PROGRAM IV

William Grant Still is a deeply, unpretentiously religious man. A program of his works directly reflecting this is a contagious experience for the listener.

Archaic Ritual suggests voodoo rituals. There is a primitive chant of priests, a dance before the altar, a moment of possession by the spirits.

The compositions from the West Indies and from North America are all arrangements of authentic folk material, giving a different viewpoint, albeit reverent, to the usually accepted religious mood.

The Voice of the Lord is a moving setting of Psalm 29, Hebraic in feeling. Commissioned by the Park Avenue Synagogue.

A Psalm for the Living is an anthem based on the idea that God is not remote but living amongst us. There are no departures in form; the content and message are uppermost. An attractive melody.

All That I Am is a tiny piece written for church use—a hymn expressing deep reverence for God.

Poem for Orchestra has already appeared in program #1. Here it is placed in a new context as a "religious" work. In programming, should it already have been heard, conclude the religious group by repositioning *A Psalm for the Living* at the end of this program.

PROGRAM IV

Religious Works for Orchestra and Chorus

Duration

(1946) *Archaic Ritual* 20
         for symphony orchestra

(1941) *Ah, La Sa Wu!*, Ancient African Melody
         from Fox Hill 1
      Hela Grand Pere, Rada Chant
         from Haiti 1
         for chorus, piano and drums

(1937/
1941) *Three Reverent Negro Spirituals* 10
         a. Keep Me From Sinking Down
         b. Lord, I Want to be a Christian
         c. Here's One
             for chorus and piano

(1961) *Three Rhythmic Spirituals* 9
         a. Lord, I Looked Down the Road
         b. Hard Trials
         c. Holy Spirit, Don't You Leave Me
             for chorus and piano

(1946) *The Voice of the Lord* (Psalm 29) 5
         for tenor soloist, chorus and piano

(1954) *A Psalm for the Living* 10
         for chorus and orchestra

(1965) *All That I Am* 2
         for chorus and orchestra

(1944) *Poem for Orchestra* 15
         for symphony orchestra

NOTES: PROGRAM V

This program contains works listed on previous programs, but here they appear in other arrangements.

Still's early band writing was in the style of the bands usually heard in the U.S. When he later heard the West Point band and recognized its orchestral qualities, he composed the *Folk Suite* in the broader idiom. These latter works reflect Still's skill as an orchestrator. Their performance requires an excellent concert band.

The organ works were written on commission. They are offertory pieces, quiet and without bombast. *Summerland* (originally for piano) was arranged for organ by Edouard Vies-Berger, and its title and style are intended to indicate a poetic vision of heaven.

Still's works for chorus show the same variety and concerns as do his other writings. *Lost Continent,* for example, conjures up the legendary world of Mu. Music for the songs of worship, dance, yearning and magic (which give it musical form) was written first. Still then created the lost language out of syllables. Although there are no real words, when sung the syllables and music seem to have been born together. *Lost Continent, Psalm for the Living* and *Plain-Chant for America* may be performed with a simple piano accompaniment, or with orchestral accompaniment.

PROGRAM V

Works for Band, Organ and Chorus

Duration

Band

(1945) *From the Delta* 8

(1967) *The Little Red Schoolhouse* 15

(1963) *Folk Suite* 8

(1951) *To You America* 11

Organ

(1962) *Reverie* 3

(1963) *Elegie* 3

(1936) *Summerland* 3

Chorus

(1948) *The Lost Continent* 15

(1954) *Psalm for the Living* 10

(1941) *Plain-Chant for America* 10

NOTES: PROGRAM VI

Troubled Island had its premiere under the City Center Opera Company of New York. While it was destined for success, it never had its full run and should be redone today. Its Haitian theme is worked out in good, solid, melodic music. Folk passages interweave with poetic and dramatic writing. Still says it is a "heavy show", and expensive to do, but he knows that when the time is right, it will be rediscovered.

Other operatic works by Still await performance. Chief among them are *Costaso*, a California folk opera, and the major *Minette Fontaine*, an opera about an opera singer, set in New Orleans.

PROGRAM VI

Operatic Work

Duration

(1941) *TROUBLED ISLAND* 120

Opera in 3 acts, based on the life of Haiti's first Emperor, Jean Jacques Dessalines.

4 stage sets, chorus, full orchestra, 8 vocal soloists, ballet.

NOTES: PROGRAM VII

The early piano works of Still show him under the influence of his teacher, Edgar Varese, whom he credits with broadening his horizons. Not to represent this phase of Still's explorations is to miss the serious European avant-gardism which he practiced and ultimately discarded in favor of his ethnic and more basically lyrical heritage. *Kaintuck* is an example of the latter.

Songs of Separation, a bi-lingual cycle, based on the texts of various American Negro and Haitian poets, represents Still's power and subtlety with the art song.

Kaintuck is a two piano arrangement made from the piano and orchestra score. Goossens, Hanson and Klemperer have all conducted it. A Southern *Nights in the Gardens of Spain,* written by Still in lieu of a piano concerto. Substantial piano part but not virtuosistic, rather a poem for piano and orchestra. Intended to be played lyrically, the work suggests aspects of the varied scenery on the Cincinnati to Lexington route.

Regarding the chamber works: *Incantation and Dance* is written for oboe and piano. In Still's personal idiom, the work contains no folk materials. *Miniatures* is just the reverse—arrangements of five folk tunes from the Western Hemisphere—North and South American. Still's settings impose little, and bring out the essential character of the material. *Vignettes* develops Inca melodies. *Danzas de Panama* are folk things from various sources: Indian, Negro, Spanish.

PROGRAM VII

Songs and Varied Chamber Works

Duration

Piano

(1936) *Three Visions* 11

(1939) *Seven Traceries* 17

(1944) *Bells* 6

Voice and Piano

(1949) *Songs of Separation* 12

Two Pianos

(1935) *Kaintuck* 13

Chamber Music

(1945) *Incantation and Dance* 5

(1948) *Miniatures* 12

(1962) *Vignettes* 12

(1948) *Danzas de Panama* 15

All of William Grant Still's violin works—whether composed or arranged—were inspired by Louis and Annette Kaufman, who introduced them. The *Suite for Violin* is racial, though on original themes, because it portrays musically the works of three outstanding Negro artists. In sharp contrast is *Pastorela*, a California poem; and the arrangements of Mr. Still's own *Summerland* and *Carmela*, a folk melody from early California. The arrangements of the Lenox Avenue *Blues* and *Here's One* were made by Louis Kaufman.

PROGRAM VIII

Violin Works

	Duration
(1943) *Suite for Violin*	11
(1936) *Summerland*	4
(1946) *Pastorela*	9
(1937) *Blues* (from Lenox Avenue)	3

Folk Music from North America

(1962) 1. *Carmela*	2
(1941) 2. *Here's One*	2

NOTES: PROGRAM IX

This program concentrates on the American aspect of William Grant Still's work. *The American Scene* is a series of five suites for young Americans, each suite containing three sections, each of which describes a different locale in the United States. Excerpts from these suites may be performed, in the event that a performance of the entire group would be too long.

Lenox Avenue, of course, is racial because it depicts street scenes in New York's Harlem.

Highway 1, U.S.A. is a short opera, inexpensive to produce, also with an American setting and flavor. It has had several successful performances, some by college students.

PROGRAM IX

Radio Music and Stage Works

Duration

(1957) *The American Scene* 45

(1937) *Lenox Avenue* (Concert Version) 27

(1962) *Highway 1, U.S.A.* 60

An incident in the life of an American family, set in a filling station near the highway.

1 stage set, chorus, reduced orchestra, 4 vocal soloists.

NOTES: PROGRAM X

Since this program consists entirely of composed works (no folk material) and is also what might be termed all "program" music, descriptive of different themes, it gives a comprehensive view of the wide range of Mr. Still's imagination, from the regional descriptive music such as *Old California* and *Dismal Swamp* to the African overtones in *Ennanga*, the Spiritual-like melodies in the little requiem for the colored soldiers (*In Memoriam*), the vision of a land free of turmoil in *The Peaceful Land*, and the haunting *Symphony #5*, based on the composer's concept of the Western Hemisphere.

The Poem which precedes the "Western Hemisphere" *Symphony #5* is as follows:

> One day in eternity has come to its close. A mighty civilization has begun, come to a climax, and declined. In the darkness, the past is swept away. When the new day dawns, the lands of the Western Hemisphere are raised from the bosom of the Atlantic. They are endowed by the Great Intelligence who created them and who controls their destiny with virtues unlike any that have gone before: qualities which will find counterparts in the characters of the men who will inhabit them eventually, and who will make them the abode of freedoms, of friendship, of the sharing of resources and achievements of the mind and of the spirit. These are our fellow-Americans in Latin America, Canada and the islands of the Western Seas, who are today working with us to convert our ideals into realities.

PROGRAM X

Orchestral Works

Duration

(1941) *Old California* 10

(1936) *Dismal Swamp* 15

(1956) *Ennanga* 15
(with harp soloist)

(1943) *In Memoriam* 6

(1960) *The Peaceful Land* 9

(1945) *Symphony #5* 25

R. B. H.

ABOUT THE CONTRIBUTORS

Dr. Robert Bartlett Haas

Editor of this volume and Director of the Department of Arts and Humanities, University Extension, UCLA, is active in several phases of the arts in California. He has numerous and unusual publications—translations from the German on Kurt Schwitters, books and articles about Psychodrama, pioneer California photographers, textiles and the visual arts. Recently his book, *A Primer for the Gradual Understanding of Gertrude Stein,* has been published by the Black Sparrow Press. His first acquaintance with the music of William Grant Still was made during his high school years in Stockton, California—an interest which he has maintained until today.

Dr. Frederick D. Hall

Composer, instrumentalist, conductor and music educator. One of the most distinguished figures in Afro-American music. Born December 14, 1898 in Atlanta, George and educated in American universities as well as in the Royal College of Music in London, he has since been director of music in several colleges in the South, most recently Dillard University in New Orleans. He is a member of the American Guild of Organists and a fellow of the Royal Anthropological Institution in recognition of his studies of the African origins of some American Negro music.

Dr. Howard Hanson

Dean of American composers, also conductor and leading music educator in the United States. First and still strongest sponsor of serious American music through his now-famous American Composers' Concerts at the Eastman School of Music, which he directed until his recent retirement. Born October 28, 1896 in Wahoo, Nebraska.

Annette Kaufman

The pianist-wife of Louis Kaufman has been his accompanist in concerts in North and South America and Europe, and his associate in research. Her teachers were James Friskin in New York City and Madame Jeanne Blancard, assistant to Alfred Cortot, at the Ecole Normale in Paris, France.

Louis Kaufman

The *New York Times* has called him a "violinists' violinist and a musicians' musician". He has appeared as soloist with many of the major symphony orchestras and has received the Naumburg Award and the Loeb Prize in New York City for performances, the "Grand Prix du Disque" in France for his recording of Vivaldi's "Four Seasons" concerti and a Citation from the Los Angeles Chapter of the National Association of American Composers and Conductors for his recordings and performances of works by Samuel Barber, Robert Russell Bennett, Aaron Copland, Everett Helm, Quincy Porter, Walter Piston, Robert McBride, and William Grant Still. His recordings range from the first 12 concertos written by Guiseppe Torelli and 36 concerti of Antonio Vivaldi to contemporary works by Toch, Milhaud, Copland and Bennett.

PAUL H. SLATTERY

Instrumental music instructor in the public schools of Jackson and, at present, Cupertino, California. Born in San Francisco, California on April 5, 1927. Attended St. Anselm's, Tamalpais High School, and College of Marin. A.B. and B.M. from College of the Pacific (now University of the Pacific). M.A. from San Jose State College in 1969. A portion of the Master's Thesis is used in this publication. Activities include choir director.

DR. WILLIAM GRANT STILL

Often called the Dean of American Negro composers. Born May 11, 1895 in Woodville, Mississippi, his career has spanned more than half a century in serious and commercial American music. Self-taught in orchestration, he was an innovator in that field for radio, and was a pioneer in elevating the Negro musical idiom to symphonic status. In the area of human relations he was also outstanding, becoming the first Negro to conduct a white radio orchestra in New York, first to write a symphony which was performed, first to have an opera produced by a major opera company in the United States, first to conduct a major symphony orchestra in the United States (1936) and first to conduct a major symphony orchestra in the Deep South (1955). His compositions, in many different media, place him among the top composers of serious music in America.

VERNA ARVEY (Mrs. William Grant Still)

Pianist, journalist, largely for publications devoted to music and the dance. Author of the book, *Choreographic Music*, published in the early forties by Dutton. Also librettist for most of William Grant Still's operas and recent vocal works. Born February 16, 1910 in Los Angeles, California.

201

ACKNOWLEDGEMENTS

Sources: MY ARKANSAS BOYHOOD, The Arkansas Historical Quarterly: Autumn, 1967. WITH HIS ROOTS IN THE SOIL, The International Musician: July, 1963. MEMO FOR MUSICOLOGISTS, Music Journal: November, 1969. STILL OPERA POINTS THE WAY, Music Forum and Digest: August, 1949. MODERN COMPOSERS HAVE LOST THEIR AUDIENCE: WHY?, Australian Musical News: July, 1956. AN AFRO-AMERICAN COMPOSER'S VIEWPOINT, American Composers on American Music: Stanford University Press: 1933. HORIZONS UNLIMITED, A lecture delivered at UCLA: November 21, 1957. A COMPOSER'S VIEWPOINT, From the Dominique deLerma book, "Black Music in our Culture": Ohio, Kent State University Press: 1970. Text of a speech delivered at the 1969 Indiana University Seminar on Black Music.

Authorship: Out of regard for the overall unity of this volume, the writers have chosen not to sign their individual contributions in the text, but rather to indicate this with their initials. Specific authorship may easily be determined by comparing these initials with the biographical listing at the end of the book.

Musical Examples: Composer's own script.

Typing of the manuscript: Hazel Young and Sharon Arendes.

Photographs: From the collection of Mr. & Mrs. William Grant Still.

*Printed July 1972 in Santa Barbara for
the Black Sparrow Press by Noel Young.
Design by Barbara Martin. The regular
edition is limited to 1000 hardcover copies.
100 special copies handbound in boards by
Earle Gray have been numbered & signed
by William Grant Still.*